Up Up and Array!

Dynamic Array Formulas for Excel 365 and Beyond

Abbott Ira Katz

Apress®

Up Up and Array!: Dynamic Array Formulas for Excel 365 and Beyond

Abbott Ira Katz
Edgware, UK

ISBN-13 (pbk): 978-1-4842-8965-5
https://doi.org/10.1007/978-1-4842-8966-2

ISBN-13 (electronic): 978-1-4842-8966-2

Managing Director, Apress Media LLC: Welmoed Spahr
Acquisitions Editor: Joan Murray
Development Editor: Laura Berendson
Coordinating Editor: Jill Balzano

Cover Photo by Clem Onojeghuo on Unsplash

Distributed to the book trade worldwide by Springer Science+Business Media LLC, 1 New York Plaza, Suite 4600, New York, NY 10004. Phone 1-800-SPRINGER, fax (201) 348-4505, e-mail orders-ny@springer-sbm.com, or visit www.springeronline.com. Apress Media, LLC is a California LLC and the sole member (owner) is Springer Science + Business Media Finance Inc (SSBM Finance Inc). SSBM Finance Inc is a **Delaware** corporation.

For information on translations, please e-mail booktranslations@springernature.com; for reprint, paperback, or audio rights, please e-mail bookpermissions@springernature.com.

Apress titles may be purchased in bulk for academic, corporate, or promotional use. eBook versions and licenses are also available for most titles. For more information, reference our Print and eBook Bulk Sales web page at http://www.apress.com/bulk-sales.

Any source code or other supplementary material referenced by the author in this book is available to readers on GitHub (https://github.com/Apress). For more detailed information, please visit http://www.apress.com/source-code.

Printed on acid-free paper

Dedicated to spreadsheet users ready to take the next step.

Table of Contents

About the Author

Abbott Ira Katz is a native New Yorker living in London. He's been teaching Excel for 25 years, exploring the application with learners on both sides of the Atlantic. He has authored two previous Apress books on Excel – *Microsoft Excel 2010* and *Excel 2010 Made Simple* – wrote the spreadsheetjournalism.com blog, and has contributed Excel-themed pieces to datajournalism.com, the Irish Tech News, datadrivenjournalism.net, and the baseball journal *By the Numbers*. His work with spreadsheets has been cited by *The Guardian*, *The Wall Street Journal*, the Freakonomic blog, and the Excel expert Chandoo, and he gave an Excel-driven, five-session workshop on Data Stories at Sciences Po University in Paris in 2018. Abbott has a doctorate in sociology from SUNY Stony Brook. The idea for a book on dynamic array functions springs from a sense that the take-up of these potent tools remains small, and that large numbers of spreadsheet users remain unaware of their capacity for facilitating, enhancing, and enabling a myriad of wide-ranging tasks.

About the Technical Reviewer

Mikey Bronowski is a data enthusiast with a mathematics background who has been working with SQL Server for over 16 years. He works as a Data Platform Architect at datamasterminds.io and is a Microsoft Data Platform MVP and Microsoft Certified Trainer with a couple of certificates, sharing knowledge at Bronowski.it.

In the past, Mikey was a Poland Data Community member, and is now a proud UK Data Platform active member and SotonDataCloud.org leader.

He spends his free time freezing behind the camera.

Acknowledgments

Don't be fooled by the name on the jacket. Unless you're self-publishing, a book is by necessity a team effort, and a number of individuals contributed to the process of delivering this book from their capable hands to yours, or your screen. This estimable cadre includes:

My wife Marsha, who allowed me to retreat sufficiently far into the background in order to write what you're now reading;

Joan Murray, who started me on my journey;

Jill Balzano, whose unfailingly congenial counsel and assistance accompanied me en route;

Angel Michael Dhanaraj and her typesetting team;

Jonathan Gennick, for his redoutable production oversight, and

Mikey Bronowski, whose eagle-eyed search through the text and its myriad of formulas saved me from error and embarrassment on a number of occasions.

They all had a part in what's right about the book; I'll take the hit for what isn't.

Introduction

It's been four years since Microsoft Excel introduced a set of functions for Excel 365 that promoted a new way of thinking about and writing formulas. Called dynamic array functions, they infused formulas with a radically new potency: for the first time, a single Excel formula could unleash results across multiple cells.

Thus, it became possible to write a formula such as

=SEQUENCE(100)

by which a series of consecutive values, 1 through 100, populated 100 consecutive cells plunging down a column.

But that's just for starters. This formula, for example:

=FILTER(Sales,Salesperson=B6)

identifies all the entries in a field – Salesperson – that features a salesperson's name posted in cell B6, and returns all the records from a dataset called Sales bearing that name – even if the results number in the thousands. The formula count: one. The formula-writing potential: close to limitless.

And Excel hasn't restricted dynamic array capability to its newest functions; in fact, most of its *existing* functions now sport multi-cell capability as well, a point that *Up Up and Array!* takes pains to stress.

Now while it's true that Microsoft broke the news about dynamic arrays in September 2018, they may have caught up with your PC a good deal later than that. My set was installed – after having been stalled – in January 2020, for example. But no matter. If you're an Excel 365 subscriber you've had dynamic array capability for some time now, and this book seeks to familiarize you with the functions and their vast promise for empowering and streamlining the formulas you write – and the formulas you didn't realize you *could* write.

Excel has released its current complement of dynamic array functions in two waves: the first set of six – SEQUENCE, UNIQUE, SORT, SORTBY, FILTER, and RANDARRAY (along with the @ function you'll use most sparingly, if at all; but there's more about it in the book) dating from that 2018 inception point – and a later collection of 14 brought out earlier this year that continue to be rolled out to 365 users as of this writing.

But note that while the original six *are* likewise available to owners of Excel 2021, Microsoft has no current plan to implement the newer 14 to that version – at least as of now (remember that Excel 2021 offers itself as an as-is application, and can't receive uploaded updates). One assumes that 2021 or its successor will acquire the new functions sooner or later, but who knows? By then it may be called Excel 2023.

Up Up and Array! commences by addressing the tricky definitional issue of the term array, and then proceeds to recount some of the defining features of array formulas, both past and present. It moves on to detail the new functions themselves, supplementing the exposition with numerous examples and illustrative screenshots. And you can click through those examples via the practice files stored here: `https://github.com/Apress`.

Up Up and Array! is a concise work devoted specifically to the workings of dynamic array functions and the new possibilities for formula writing they encourage. It's my hope that as a result, you'll come to appreciate, and perhaps even be inspired, by the decidedly cool things they – and you – can do.

Abbott Ira Katz

CHAPTER 1

What's an Array, Anyway?

Good question. That term – array – has secured a foothold in all sorts of computing vocabularies and has made a series of guest appearances in the dictionaries of other scientific domains as well. But while that's all very nice, you want to know what arrays mean for the Excel user, and how that understanding can add value – quite a bit of value – to your work with spreadsheets.

A Working Definition

Defining spreadsheet arrays is an assignment that brings with it bad news and good news. The bad news is that definitions of spreadsheet arrays vary. It seems, for example, that some writers all but equate the terms range and array. Indeed – a Microsoft website asserts that "You can think of an array as a row or column of values, or a combination of rows and columns of values," and that sure sounds like a range to me, and leaves me none the wiser; and a Google site describes array in almost the same terms. But because "range" seems so often to be twinned with "array," we can ask the obvious question: Why then do we need *both* of them? And just to make sure you're paying attention, Excel sometimes trots out "vector," too.

Indeed, Excel savant Liam Bastick (`https://www.accountingweb.co.uk/tech/excel/xlookup-and-xmatch-two-new-x-men-for-excel`) states that "An array is a collection of cells consisting of at least two rows and at least two columns," while maintaining that a vector "is a collection of cells across just one row…or down just one column…" Hmmm.

On the other hand, Mike Girvin, author of the near-legendary tome on array formulas *Ctrl-Shift-Enter* (a volume that has since slipped into near-obsolescence, though the significance of its title will become clearer as we proceed), goes small and calls an array "a collection of two or more items." I can't say that I'm edified. And for the late spreadsheet master Chip Pearson, an array is a series of values (`http://www.cpearson.com/excel/ArrayFormulas.aspx`), but you're getting the idea.

1

© Abbott Ira Katz 2023
A. I. Katz, *Up Up and Array!*, https://doi.org/10.1007/978-1-4842-8966-2_1

But time for the good news: Confusion notwithstanding, none of this will stand in the way of your ability to master array formulas. Once you get up and running with the formulas, you'll be able to relegate the definitional details to mere barroom debate – though if you can track down a bar in which the regulars actually argue about array formulas, please take me there; the next round will be on me.

So in the interests of cutting to the chase, let's propose the following take: for starters, an array is a collection of values that appear in a formula, to be subjected to whatever operation the formula chooses to perform. Begin with an elementary illustration: suppose I enter the values 1, 2, and 3 in cells A1:A3, and total them via a SUM function positioned in A4. If I click on A4, and in turn click the Insert Function button (the fx indicator stationed to the left of the Formula Bar) that exposes the innards of a formula, I'll see what is shown in Figure 1-1.

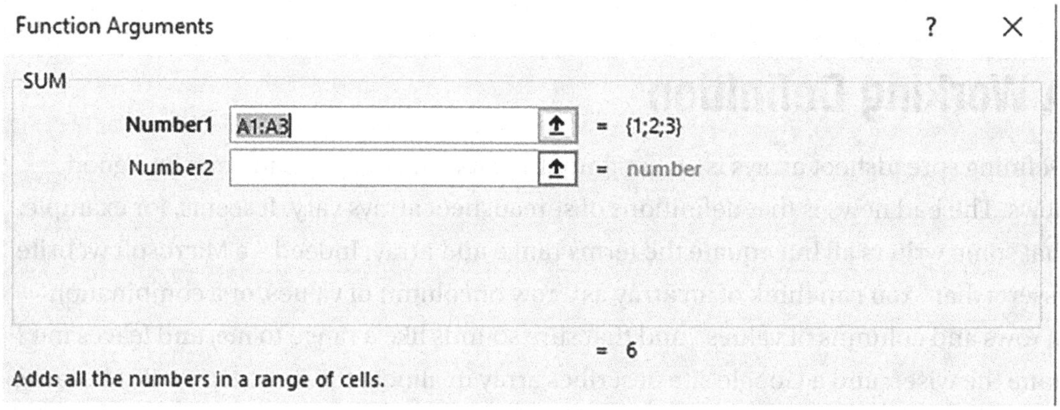

Figure 1-1. Face to face with an array

You're looking at an array – our values 1, 2, and 3, surrounded by the hallmark brackets that accompany an array expression. The sum itself in the lower reaches of the screenshot – 6 – is bracket-free, because among other things an array must comprise at least two values (but more about that later). And had I replaced SUM with an AVERAGE, or MAX, or COUNT function and proceeded to tick the fx button again, we'd discover that the resulting array would appear precisely as we see it above – {1,2,3}.

Now let's consider another example. Suppose I construct a standard VLOOKUP function, one that seeks to look up student grades for either of two subjects in the range A1:C11 as per Figure 1-2.

name	soc	phil
Bill	75	90
Dana	55	68
Ed	61	38
Jack	34	80
Jane	36	83
Hortense	41	85
Paul	71	59
Ted	66	66
Ulysses	59	52
Wanda	84	97

Figure 1-2. *Testing, testing: student exam grades to be looked up*

After entering any student's name in I1 and writing a VLOOKUP formula in I3 that looks up the student's grade for the philosophy exam (column 3 of the lookup range):

$$=VLOOKUP(I1,A1:C11,3,0)$$

I'll return to I3 and once again click the fx button. We'll see the following, in Figure 1-3.

Function Arguments		? ✕
VLOOKUP		
Lookup_value	I1	= "Dana"
Table_array	A1:d11	= {"name","soc","phil";"Bill",75,90;"Dana"
Col_index_num	3	= 3
Range_lookup	0	= FALSE
		= 68

Looks for a value in the leftmost column of a table, and then returns a value in the same row from a column you specify. By default, the table must be sorted in an ascending order.

Table_array   is a table of text, numbers, or logical values, in which data is retrieved. Table_array can be a reference to a range or a range name.

Figure 1-3. *Another array, this one produced by a VLOOKUP formula*

Here we encounter a subtle difference from the array captured by our SUM example. Look closely, and you'll note the semicolon that separates the entries "phil" and "Bill," as well as "90" and "Dana." That bit of punctuation signals that both "Bill" and "Dana" appear in new *rows* in what Microsoft here insists on calling the table array (I told you definitions vary), i.e., "Bill" immediately follows "phil" in the array, but appears in the next row in the worksheet (review Figure 1-2). We've thus learned a pair of rules about array notation: a comma interposed between array values means they share the same row, while a semicolon indicates that the values break at the semicolon and swing down into a new row in the worksheet – kind of an array word wrap.

Now for Something Different

But in both of our cases – SUM and VLOOKUP – we've seen that the formulas have simply grabbed the values from their respective cells in the worksheet and remade them into arrays, readying them for whatever function on which the user decides. But – and this is a big but – sometimes an array consists of values that haven't been drawn from the spreadsheet, but have been *produced by the formula itself.*

Here's what I mean. Suppose I want to calculate the number of characters populating a range of words, the kind of character count you'd normally see in a word processor. Let's try these words, again inhabiting A1:A3 (Figure 1-4).

| Today |
| is |
| Thursday |

Figure 1-4. *Cast of characters: words ready for a character count*

In A4 we'll write the following formula (to be explained in greater detail at a later point):

=SUM(LEN(A1:A3))

If you're typing along with me, you'll understand that the result, 15, registers the count of all the characters contributing to our three words; but now revisit that fx button, click it, and you'll see the following in Figure 1-5.

Function Arguments		?	×
SUM			
Number1	LEN(A1:A3)	⬆ = {5;2;8}	
Number2		⬆ = number	

= 15

Figure 1-5. *Three little words: the character count for each word in the range*

Unlike our previous examples, the values 5, 2, and 8 in the preceding array appear *nowhere* in the worksheet; they represent the individual character counts of the three words in our range – and they've been calculated by, and restricted to, the formula only.

What we've viewing here is an array formula, so called because the *formula itself has generated the array*. While it's true, of course, that our SUM and VLOOKUP illustrations also exhibit arrays, we've seen that those formulas simply reproduced the data in the worksheet and tossed them into the formulas. Here, the *formula builds the array internally*, and that's what we mean by an array formula: a formula that realizes multiple *results* – here, the 5, 2, and the 8.

What We Mean – and What We Don't Mean

Note again, on the other hand, that the bottom-line character count in the formula above – 15 – isn't deemed an array. To restate an earlier point, arrays consist of multiple values. Here, it's rather the intermediate results, the three character counts, that bind themselves into the array.

And don't confuse multiple results with multiple calculations. Is it possible, for example, to add a million values with the SUM function? It sure is. Remember that an Excel worksheet hands the user more than 17 billion cells to play with, so summing a paltry million of them is a walk in the park. And it's true – that formula would have to perform 999,999 calculations, factoring each successive cell value into the result. But that massive process will nevertheless leave us with but *one* result – the overall total, deposited into one cell.

But an array formula cooks up a batch of *individual, stand-alone results*, again in our character-count case 5, 2, and 8. That trio of values sits side by side in the waiting room of the formula until some finalizing action – in our case SUM – parachutes the total of 15 into a single cell. But the three distinct results came first, and they came from the formula.

By way of additional example, we could write this array formula instead:

$$=AVERAGE(LEN(A1:A3))$$

in which case its result – 5 – will again find its way into its cell. But here too, the average is derived from the array that's been manufactured by the formula: 5, 2, and 8.

Note   Dave Bruns' treatment (`https://exceljet.net/glossary/array`) of "array" verges close to the view advanced here.

Introducing…Dynamic Arrays

Now for the next big point. The two array formulas we've introduced – the ones computing the sum of the characters of three words and the average character-per-word – are the kind that can in fact be written in *any* version of Excel. And that raises an important introductory point. While you may be new to array formulas, array formulas aren't new to Excel; they've occupied a musty, seldom-visited corner in Excel's storeroom of tools for many years, even if a great many Excel users have been afraid to poke around that corner.

But with the rollout of Office 365 came a radical new development. The way in which array formulas – now labeled dynamic arrays – are written was dramatically retooled and accompanied, you'll be happy to know, by a significant boost in their ease of use.

So What's New?

To understand what's new about arrays in Office 365, let's modify the character-summing formula that's occupied us for the last few pages. Returning to the three words we've posted to A1:A3, enter the following in B1:

$$=LEN(A1:A3)$$

That is, we've merely replicated our original SUM formula, minus the SUM. Figure 1-6 shows what you should see.

Today	5
is	2
Thursday	8

Figure 1-6. *Character count, this time word by word*

Again, the character count of each word is returned; but while we've already been there and done that, here the formula *delivers its array to cells in the worksheet.* For the first time, the formula in B1 has pitched its three results into the B column; and had we been asked to character-count 1000 words bolting down the A column instead, this formula

$$=LEN(A1:A1000)$$

would have done just that. And that's new for Excel. Try the above formulas in a pre-365 version of the application, and you'll discover you can't get there from here. Rather, what you *will* discover, for example, is that writing =LEN(A1:A3) in cell B1 in the older versions will dispatch only *one* result – 5 – to B1, for example, the length of the word in A1. That's because formulas in pre-365 Excel were incapable of depositing multiple results in multiple cells, a shortcoming called implicit intersection about which we'll learn a bit more later.

The one-formula/multi-cell capability of dynamic arrays is new – and big. It greatly streamlines the formula writing process and, with a bit of imagination, empowers the user to productively apply arrays across an enormous swath of data-manipulating tasks, as we hope to demonstrate.

And so to summarize the plot thus far: While by definition, all array formulas can turn out multiple results, dynamic array formulas can *transmit those results to cells in the worksheet,* through a process Excel calls *spilling.*

Moreover, if the range(s) referenced by a dynamic array formula changes, the number of cells that spills – that is, the new result of the now-rewritten formula – will also immediately change. And that's what's dynamic about them. And don't worry: plenty of examples are to follow.

And to further these ends, Excel has brought out a fleet of dynamic array functions poised to supercharge your formulas with that multi-cell firepower – and they're pretty easy to write, too. In fact, two batches of the new functions have been issued, and we mean to look at them all here – even if you don't yet have all of them.

And while it's true that much of this book is devoted to the new functions, precisely because they're new, don't let the new ones distract you from the larger point – namely, that nearly *all* of Excel's functions – for example, the old reliables like SUM, AVERAGE, VLOOKUP, MATCH, SEARCH, and many more – have been vested with dynamic array clout, too. On the one hand, it isn't our intention to expound the hundreds of pre-365 formulas in detail – that's for a different kind of book – but again we want to indicate that these too have been equipped with dynamic array functionality (for a directory of all of Excel's functions, less the newest ones just announced, look here).

This book, then, isn't only about the new tools enlarging Excel's inventory; it's really about Excel, and how it's changed, and how it'll change the way you work.

Some Points to Bear in Mind

Before we begin to describe the workings of dynamic array formulas, let's offer a few more preliminaries. First, this book can't hope or presume to tell you everything there is to know about dynamic arrays. After all, given their immense potential, I'm not sure that objective is even possible, and even if it was it would call for a book so enormous you wouldn't want to read it, and I wouldn't want to write it. As every halfway-experienced Excel user knows, the same spreadsheet task very often lends itself to multiple approaches, and so the techniques called upon here may well not be the only one.

Second, you'll note that most of the screen shots reveal the formulas that gave rise to the results captured in the shots. They appear courtesy of the most useful FORMULATEXT function, but these of course won't automatically materialize on your sheet if you're clicking along with me.

And finally, it's acknowledged that the examples placed before you here aren't necessarily "real-world" in character, ones that'll solve that pertinacious spreadsheet problem at work that's knocked your resident guru for a loop. Rather, the plan is to detail how the functions, and formulas founded upon those functions, are written, and what they actually do – without any necessary regard for actual, need-to-do tasks.

CHAPTER 2

Array Formula Basics

The Old and the New

Array formulas have a reputation – and it's not a particularly good one. For many spreadsheet users, they're Excel's equivalent of a dark alley at 3 in the morning; one just doesn't go there.

Why not? Possibly because array formulas ask the user to think of, and work with, ranges in a way that displaces them from their comfort zone. Every spreadsheet formula works with ranges, of course, but array formulas – both the earlier and the newer dynamic-array kind – subject the values to a different kind of collective treatment.

To exemplify that idea, let's return again to our character-count-summing array formula that featured in the previous chapter:

=SUM(LEN(A1:A3))

Now, if you knew nothing about array formulas but still needed to tabulate the number of characters populating our three-cell range, you'd write, as in Figure 2-1.

Today	5	=LEN(A1)
Is	2	=LEN(A2)
Thursday	8	=LEN(A3)
	15	=SUM(B1:B3)

Figure 2-1. *Going to great lengths: adding the lengths of words individually*

Here we're viewing what I call the by-the-book means for achieving the character count. We've written a LEN function in B1 for the word in A1, copied that formula down the B column on an as-needed basis, and concluded the process by writing a SUM formula that adds all the counts. If our range consisted of 1000 words, then, we'd have to copy the formula in B1 999 times down B and report the count with SUM:

© Abbott Ira Katz 2023
A. I. Katz, *Up Up and Array!*, https://doi.org/10.1007/978-1-4842-8966-2_2

$$=SUM(A1:A1000)$$

That task, then, would require 1001 formulas.

While of course these results will be correct, the array alternative could engineer the same outcomes with exactly one formula. If you needed to calculate the total lengths of 100,000 words inundating the A column, you'd have to direct 100,001 formulas at them. The array formula count? Again, one.

The general strategy for writing an array formula would be to ask yourself how you would achieve the desired result if you'd never heard of arrays. Your answer would likely look something like the screenshot in Figure 2-1. You then need to ask yourself how all that activity could be crammed into a single formula, because here you want to account for all the character lengths of the words in *one expression*, for example,

$$=LEN(A1:A3)$$

And you'd then surround, or wrap, that formula with the SUM function.

This array formula carries out two operations – the cell-by-cell length calculations as well as their overall sum – and again, within the space of one formula. It's this way of thinking, in which the formula is made to multitask with multiple values, that may be new to you, but a bit of reflection about the array process along with some directed practice will serve you well.

Remember again, however, that this dynamic array formula

$$=LEN(A1:A3)$$

freed of SUM, will release its results into *multiple* cells. It's as if the SUM function locks its data inside the formula, forcing a single aggregated result into a single cell.

An Important Reminder

And that reminds us of an important general rule: if an array formula evaluates to a one-celled result, you should be able to write it in a pre-365 iteration of Excel. But a *multi-cell* return in the worksheet *requires 365 or beyond*. Thus, to repeat, this array formula

$$=SUM(LEN(A1:A3))$$

can be written in any version of Excel, because it yields one result – the sum of the word lengths. But this formula

$$=LEN(A1:A3)$$

can only be successfully written in Excel 365 or later, because it will lodge its results in multiple cells.

Remembrance of Keystrokes Past

And those reminders recall another reason why so many Excel users crossed the street when they saw an array formula coming. If a user mustered the courage to actually write one of them in the bygone, pre-365 days, the array formula was instated in its cell not via a simple tap of the Enter key, but by banging out a fearsome triad of keystrokes instead: Ctrl-Shift-Enter.

That legendary sequence (which accounts for Mike Girvin's book title), which as of this writing remains a staple of array formulas in Google Sheets, ordered the formula to do something against its better nature – namely, pump out an internal array of values instead of the minimalist, single-celled output it was programmed to do. LEN was designed, after all, for this

=LEN(A1)

And not this

=LEN(A1:A3)

But Ctrl-Shift-Enter forced, or as the geeks like to put it, coerced, formulas to suppress their just-one-result instinct and make room for multiple results instead – even if for first-generation array formulas those results were confined to the formulas themselves. That process is called *lifting*, and is integral to array formulas; but more to the point, lifting now serves as Excel's *default* formula capability. In any case, we'll have more to say about lifting later.

But there was still more back then to make the would-be array formula writer break into a cold sweat. Once the formula was completed and nestled safely in its cell, the result would look like this:

{=SUM(LEN(A1:A3))}

The brackets, those squiggly formations we've seen attaching to arrays in the inner recesses of formulas, here showed up in actual formulas *in their cells*, doubtless triggering the same question in the minds of countless Excel users: what in the world are *those*?

That, too, was a good question, once upon a time. But not to worry, with the advent of dynamic arrays, both Ctrl-Shift-Enter and the brackets flanking array formulas have been abolished, and if you never knew about them to begin with, you're in luck – there's nothing for you to unlearn. They're gone. Nowadays, every Excel formula, array or otherwise, springs into action with Enter and nothing more. As for the brackets, more need be said, but rest assured: you won't see them clamped around formulas in their cells.

Note   A handful of pre-365 formulas, most notably SUMPRODUCT, were empowered with native array formula status and so only required the user to press the Enter key. But even SUMPRODUCT could still only deliver its result to a single cell.

Back to the Basics

Now in the interests of battening down your array skills, consider these additional array examples. Figure 2-1 sports four instances of the FORMULATEXT function, written in cells C1:C4. These capture the formulas entered in B1:B4, and again – the by-the-book means for implementing them would ask us to write the first instance of FORMULATEXT in C1, and then copy it down the following three cells. By now, you may be able to predict what the dynamic array alternative looks like. In C1 simply enter

=FORMULATEXT(C1:C4)

Press Enter, and the deed is done. One formula, multiple instances of FORMULATEXT (again, "spilling"), and no brackets. Just remember that you can't write this one in earlier versions of Excel.

And that spilled range bears a closer look. We've written the formula in C1, and of course a click on that cell will disclose what we've written there. But click on C2 and the same formula will appear, but dimly – in a kind of shadow emanation of the original. You won't be able to delete C2, or any cell that's been spilled by the source formula. Delete C1 – the cell featuring the actual formula, on the other hand – and the entire spill range will vanish.

Now here's an even simpler example, but again, one you can't emulate in past versions. If you key in a set of names down a column, for example, Figure 2-2,

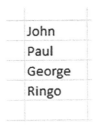

Figure 2-2. *A quartet of values*

and call this diminutive range say, Beatles, I can enter

=Beatles

anywhere in the worksheet (or any other sheet in the workbook, by default), and immediately spill those names down its column.

That's pure dynamic arraying at work, and that kind of range can offer to the thoughtful user more than gimmickry. A teacher could list all her student names in a range and call it Class, and by typing =Class anywhere else in the workbook could immediately summon all the names for grading, attendance, or any other administrative purpose. A work supervisor could do the same with a staff roster; type the range name, and the roster appears.

And by way of review of our discussion in Chapter 1, be reminded that writing =Beatles in pre-365 Excel and tapping Enter would result in "John" – and *only* John.

Now for the record, a multi-cell workaround of sorts *did* avail itself to the pre-365 generation. If I were to select four cells *first,* proceed to click in the formula bar and enter =Beatles, and *then* enter Ctrl-Shift-Enter, the names of each of the Fab Four would indeed make a place for themselves, one to a cell. But that's a tricky – and inefficient – ask.

The One-Formula Grader

Now for something slightly different, let's look at a hypothetical multiple-test answer key, and compare it to the responses managed by a student in the file *Single Student Grades,* for example, as illustrated by Figure 2-3.

Quest.	Answer Key	Student
1	A	A
2	C	D
3	B	B
4	B	B
5	D	C
6	A	A
7	C	B
8	B	B
9	D	A
10	D	D

Figure 2-3. *Multi-cell multiple choice exam*

The answer key occupies B4:B13, alongside the student's replies in C4:C13. The obvious objective: to determine the student's overall grade.

Again, for a first pass at the task we could roll out the conventional, by-the-book, recipe, this time built on an IF statement. We could enter in D4

$$=IF(C4=B4,1,0)$$

What's new here is the recourse to the IF function, its formula comparing the answer to question one to the student's response: if the two match, the student receives one point; if they don't, the formula issues a zero. Next of course, we could copy the formula down the D column and cap the process by jotting a SUM function somewhere in the worksheet (Figure 2-4).

Quest.	Answer Key	Student			
1	A	A		1	=IF(C4=B4,1,0)
2	C	D		0	=IF(C5=B5,1,0)
3	B	B		1	=IF(C6=B6,1,0)
4	B	B		1	=IF(C7=B7,1,0)
5	D	C		0	=IF(C8=B8,1,0)
6	A	A		1	=IF(C9=B9,1,0)
7	C	B		0	=IF(C10=B10,1,0)
8	B	B		1	=IF(C11=B11,1,0)
9	D	A		0	=IF(C12=B12,1,0)
10	D	D		1	=IF(C13=B13,1,0)
				6	=SUM(D4:D13)

Figure 2-4. *Assessing the assessment: calculating the student's grade*

(We could go further and divide the correct-answer total by the number of exam questions, returning a score of 60%; but that step isn't necessary for our demo purposes.)

Again of course all of the above is correct, but the far shorter array route would take us here:

$$=SUM(IF(B4:B13=C4:C13,1,0))$$

And that's indeed a bit different from previous exercises. As with the character-count exercise featuring LEN, SUM wraps itself around an inner function, in this case IF; but here, and unlike LEN, the IF statement repeatedly appraises each *pair* of values making their way down their respective columns, for example, B4 with C4, B5 with C5, etc. In true array fashion, the 1's and 0's ordered up by the IF statement look like this inside the formula pictured in Figure 2-5.

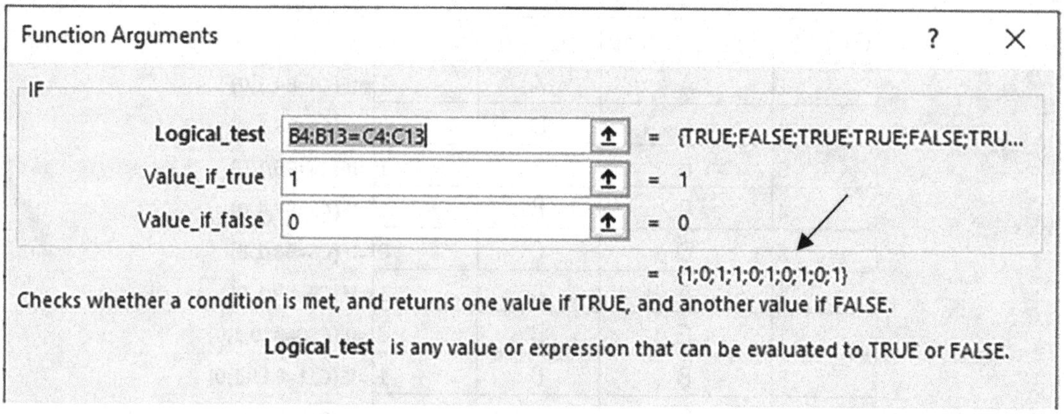

Figure 2-5. *Rights and wrongs: the test answers gathered in an array*

We've just encountered another instance of lifting – this time a special case called pairwise lifting, in which each pair of values sprawled across their rows are compared, as the formula spills its results down the D column. Our single IF formula has been made to tear up its job description and evaluate data in a *range* of cells; and those 1's and 0's – all housed in the inner sanctum of the formula – total 6, the student score.

And again, because this array formula culminates in only one result – the 6 – it's the kind that can be properly written in any version of Excel. But if we recast the formula in D4 without the embrace of SUM to

$$=IF(B4:B13=C4:C13,1,0)$$

We'll see in Figure 2-6 the following.

Quest.	Answer Key	Student		
1	A	A	1	=IF(B4:B13=C4:C13,1,0)
2	C	D	0	
3	B	B	1	
4	B	B	1	
5	D	C	0	
6	A	A	1	
7	C	B	0	
8	B	B	1	
9	D	A	0	
10	D	D	1	

Figure 2-6. *Going solo; a single IF statement calculates each grade.*

Shades of LEN(A1:A3). Here too, the IF statement – minus SUM – assigns its 1's and 0's alongside *each student answer*. Again: one formula that disgorges multiple, spilled results in their cells – an outcome only possible in Excel 365 and beyond.

The Return of the Brackets

And here's one final, introductory need-to-know. Suppose we want to write a VLOOKUP formula that would enable us to enter the name of any student in cell I9 (file: *Multiple Student Grades*) and calculate his/her average for the sociology as well the art exam, the data furnished here in cells A1:G11 (the range has been named All), and captured by Figure 2-7.

name	soc	phil	poli sci	art	physics	chem
Bill	75	90	89	72	89	79
Dana	55	68	87	47	56	50
Ed	61	38	46	36	88	66
Jack	34	80	81	56	57	64
Jane	66	83	30	72	66	56
Hortense	41	85	53	75	90	45
Paul	71	59	69	61	100	72
Ted	66	66	70	35	76	91
Ulysses	59	52	100	94	38	31
Wanda	84	97	35	52	75	86

Figure 2-7. *Six subjects in search of a formula*

Once again, we're asking a formula to step out of character – the venerable VLOOKUP had been genetically tweaked to look up the values in a single column, and now we want it to track down the values in two columns at the same time – and compute their average, besides. What would that VLOOKUP look like?

Remembering that the soc and art scores hold down columns 2 and 5 in the above lookup range, if we enter Jane in I9 and commit the VLOOKUP to cell I11, the formula reads

=AVERAGE(VLOOKUP(I9,All,{2,5}))

And we learn that Jane averaged 69 for the soc and art exams.

But there are those brackets again – the ones you thought had been permanently banished from array formulas, and tucked irretrievably into the archives. But *those* brackets were of the automatic variety, the ones that leaped into a cell whenever you put the finishing touches on an old-school array formula via the now-obsolete Ctrl-Shift-Enter. *These* brackets are user-selected and user-typed, and they throw an actual, on-the-fly array smack-dab into a formula. The values between the brackets are called *array constants,* so named because they're hard-coded, or simply typed. But don't get the wrong idea – the constants aren't inert text: here they serve to quantify the column numbers you select, and so in our case they tell VLOOKUP to search for data in columns 2 and 5. If we had entered {2,5,7}, the VLOOKUP would go ahead and compute Jane's average for soc, art, and chem: 64.67. The bottom line is this: the array constants force VLOOKUP to undertake a multi-column search for values. And once again, because all this derring-do yields a one-celled answer – the test average – our formula can be written in previous versions of Excel, but remember that if that's where you find yourself, you'll need to ratify the formula with Ctrl-Shift-Enter.

And now consider this formula variation, one that should seem rather familiar to you by now. If we pry the AVERAGE function away from the VLOOKUP, we're left with

=VLOOKUP(I9,All,{2,5,7})

This time Jane's scores for soc, art, and chem will *appear in actual, adjoining cells* (Figure 2-8).

name	soc	phil	poli sci	art	physics	chem				
Bill	75	90	89	72	89	79				
Dana	55	68	87	47	56	50				
Ed	61	38	46	36	88	66				
Jack	34	80	81	56	57	64				
Jane	66	83	30	72	66	56				
Hortense	41	85	53	75	90	45				
Paul	71	59	69	61	100	72				
Ted	66	66	70	35	76	91		Jane		
Ulysses	59	52	100	94	38	31				
Wanda	84	97	35	52	75	86		66	72	56
								=VLOOKUP(I9,All,{2,5,7})		

Figure 2-8. *It's all academic: Jane's scores in soc, art, and chem*

And again, that output confirms the multi-cell capability of dynamic array formulas. You're doubtless getting the idea.

Getting Re-oriented

But that last formula raises a new question. You'll note the horizontal alignment of Jane's three scores; but why do they proceed across a row, and not down a column instead?

In fact, we actually addressed this question in Chapter 1. Recall we observed there that if values in an array are delimited by a comma, as they in our formula here,

{2,5,7}

Then the values display themselves row-wise. If, however, we write

=VLOOKUP(I9,All,{2;5;7})

where the array values are parted by *semicolons*, Jane's scores would spill *down* a column, as in Figure 2-9.

name	soc	phil	poli sci	art	physics	chem			
Bill	75	90	89	72	89	79			
Dana	55	68	87	47	56	50			
Ed	61	38	46	36	88	66			
Jack	34	80	81	56	57	64			
Jane	66	83	30	72	66	56			
Hortense	41	85	53	75	90	45			
Paul	71	59	69	61	100	72			
Ted	66	66	70	35	76	91		Jane	
Ulysses	59	52	100	94	38	31			
Wanda	84	97	35	52	75	86		66	=VLOOKUP(I9,All,{2;5;7})
								72	
								56	

Figure 2-9. *Downward trend: Jane's scores in vertical orientation*

More of the Same

And for another, simpler example: the LARGE function identifies the nth-largest entry in a range. Thus, this expression

=LARGE(A1:A100,3)

would return the third-largest value in A1:A100. But if you wanted to elicit the top three values in that range, you could write

=LARGE(A1:A100,{1,2,3})

Again, the formula would roll out three results, one per cell; and because the array is comma-separated, they'd spill across a row.

But a Workaround Is Available

But if you just don't like those pesky brackets, here's a surprisingly obscure but easy workaround that can make your array formulas bracket-free:

Simply enter the values 2, 5, and 7 in cells I10:K10, for example, the column numbers you want to look up, the same ones that populated the brackets. Then rewrite the formula in I11:

$$=VLOOKUP(I9,All,I10:K10)$$

That new take achieves the same results, sans brackets; and if you want to change the column numbers to be looked up without editing the formula directly, just enter a different number somewhere in I10:K10.

Summing Up

We've devoted this chapter to a review of some of the essential features of first-generation array formulas, the new complement of dynamic array formulas, and what distinguishes one from the other. Note that – and again this is important – our review has run through its paces *without* having called upon any of the *new* dynamic array functions. That purposeful omission is a reminder that Microsoft's grease monkeys have installed the dynamic array engine into *most* of Excel's functions, and not merely the new ones. In the next chapter we get a bit further under the hood and explore some of the additional mechanics of the engine. No overalls required, though.

CHAPTER 3

Dynamic Arrays: Time for Some Heavy Lifting

The Spill Is Gone

True, the term "spill" – the name Excel has conferred upon its new multi-cell formula capability – suggests an episode of untidiness, like the kind of mishap I routinely inflict upon my shirt at dinner. But as we've seen in the realm of spreadsheets, spilling is a good thing indeed. Empowering one formula to dispense thousands of results to as many cells is a hugely efficient and praiseworthy feature. But there are two principal circumstances under which Excel won't allow a spill to happen.

The first: when the spill runs out of room. We can portray the problem by revisiting the test-grading illustration we framed in the previous chapter and tossing in a small complication: a bit of data adjoining the student answer to question 5 (Figure 3-1).

© Abbott Ira Katz 2023
A. I. Katz, *Up Up and Array!*, https://doi.org/10.1007/978-1-4842-8966-2_3

Quest.	Answer Key	Student	
1	A	A	
2	C	D	
3	B	B	
4	B	B	
5	D	C	text
6	A	A	
7	C	B	
8	B	B	
9	D	A	
10	D	D	

Figure 3-1. *Unwanted intrusion: text alongside answer 5*

Now if we replicate the dynamic array formula we wrote in the last chapter to cell D4,

$$=IF(B4:B13=C4:C13,1,0)$$

Figure 3-2 is what we see.

Quest.	Answer Key	Student	
1	A	A	#SPILL!
2	C	D	
3	B	B	
4	B	B	
5	D	C	text
6	A	A	
7	C	B	
8	B	B	
9	D	A	
10	D	D	

Figure 3-2. *All bottled up: the formula won't spill*

You've probably surmised what's happened, and why. The spill range's values can't assume their rightful place because the "text" entry in D8 obstructs the spill process. Spilling is an all-or-nothing proposition; if even one of the spilled values is denied entry to its cell, they all are.

If you click back on D4, and next click what Excel calls the error floatie signaled by the exclamation point, you'll see as in Figure 3-3.

◢	A	B	C	D	E
1					
2					
3	Quest.	Answer Key	Student		
4	1	A	A ⚠ ▾	#SPILL!	
5		Spill range isn't blank			
6		Help on this Error			
7		Select Obstructing Cells			
8		Show Calculation Steps		text	
9		Ignore Error			
10		Edit in Formula Bar			
11		Error Checking Options...			
12	9	D	A		
13	10	D	D		
14					
15					

Figure 3-3. Let the data flow with the Select Obstructing Cells option

First, the range earmarked for the spill – in our case, D4:D13 – is surrounded by a dotted border, as the floatie unrolls the Select Obstructing Cells option. Click it, and the cell pointer shoots to cell D8. Now that the offending entry has been pinpointed, just delete it, and the spill range now does its thing.

Of course, you could have identified the obstructing cell on your own; but remember that a single dynamic array formula can unfurl its data across multiple rows and columns at the same time, and so tracing the in-the-way cell(s) might not always be quite so straightforward and evident.

You Can't Spill on This Table

Another can't-spill-here dilemma will beset the worksheet if you write, or attempt to write, a dynamic array formula in a *table*. Sticking with our test-grade example, if I remake the grades into a table via the Ctrl-T or Insert > Table command and once again enter

=IF(B4:B13=C4:C13,1,0)

in D4, Figure 3-4 is what will happen.

Quest. ▾	Answer Key ▾	Studen ▾	Colum ▾
1	A	A	#SPILL!
2	C	D	#SPILL!
3	B	B	#SPILL!
4	B	B	#SPILL!
5	D	C	#SPILL!
6	A	A	#SPILL!
7	C	B	#SPILL!
8	B	B	#SPILL!
9	D	A	#SPILL!
10	D	D	#SPILL!

Figure 3-4. *Whole lot of spilling going on*

Note   Depending on how you write the formula here, the table might render it as =IF([Answer Key]=[@Student],1,0), but that variation won't matter for our purposes.

The spill sure isn't working here – but why?

The answer to that question had bothered me for some time, and my initial surmise was to write off a table's inability to support dynamic arrays as some design gremlin eating away at Excel's code. But then I experienced a mini-eureka moment and convinced myself that in fact, with one near-theoretical exception, tables *can't* work with dynamic array formulas.

They can't because tables and dynamic arrays operate at cross-purposes. A standard-issue, garden-variety dataset – a collection of records organized by fields – will allow the user to enter any sort of extraneous data in an adjacent column, data that needn't have anything to do with the dataset. Nothing would prevent me from entering our Beatles range in the column to the immediate right of our grades, in cell D4 as in Figure 3-5.

Quest.	Answer Key	Student	
1	A	A	John
2	C	D	Paul
3	B	B	George
4	B	B	Ringo
5	D	C	
6	A	A	
7	C	B	
8	B	B	
9	D	A	
10	D	D	

Figure 3-5. *The Beatles' next records*

But once we reinvent the data into a table, all of its rows become rigorously defined as records, and if you write an ordinary formula to the table, *it's immediately copied to all the records.* But remember that our Beatles range formula spills *four* cells, and so if the table features 100 records, and the Beatle formula and its ensuing spill range were to be copied down a table column, we'd have to contend with 400 results – and 400 cells keyed to 100 records literally doesn't compute. Because dynamic array formulas spill, their multi-cell output can't be expected to shoehorn themselves into the records of tables.

Note   There are a few other, far more obscure scenarios in which spills also won't work, that needn't concern us here.

But at the same time keep in mind that a dynamic array formula can *refer* to a table; it just can't be *entered* into one – apart from that one unlikely exception.

And that exception to the dynamic array no-table interdiction is, as noted earlier, all but theoretical. If you write a dynamic array formula that yields exactly one record, a table will accommodate it just fine – because the formula has nothing to spill. But given that the dynamic array's claim to fame is its multi-cell potency, you're not likely to write, or want to write, such a formula (thanks to Mark of Excel Off the Grid for this pointer).

The # Sign: Weighing In on Its Virtues

Among the novel features figuring in the dynamic array project is the novel way in which dynamic arrays can be referenced. Returning to the grade-assessing formula we dropped into cell D4: if we need to refer to that formula elsewhere in the worksheet, we could simply write

$$=D4\#$$

The pound-sign (or hash mark, depending on the side of the Atlantic on which you live) denotes the cell in which the dynamic array formula is actually written, and writing such a reference will duplicate the formula written to that cell, with all its spilled results.

In this case, the entry will reproduce the spill range's 1's and 0's; and this expression

$$=SUM(D4\#)$$

will naturally yield 6.

Now of course =SUM(D4:D13) could drum up the same result, but D4# boasts a few advantages: it's easier and shorter, and more to the point, the pound-sign reference will automatically register any changes to the spill range wrought by the formula.

For example, and by way of presaging the next chapter: if we ask the new dynamic array SEQUENCE function to write

$$=SEQUENCE(10)$$

in cell A3, the formula will spill a range consisting of values 1 through 10 in A3:A12. If I enter A3# somewhere else in the worksheet, the 1–10 sequence will be duplicated. If, however, I edit A3 to read

$$=SEQUENCE(30)$$

now, values 1 through 30 will zoom down cells A3:A32. But that A3#, wherever it's been written, won't miss a beat; it too will display numbers 1 through 30, accommodating the additional results spilling from the rewritten SEQUENCE formula. And

$$=COUNT(A3\#)$$

will output 30. But here, even though the COUNT formula is of the one-result type, it *can't* be written in previous Excel versions – because those versions have neither the SEQUENCE function nor the pound sign option.

Raising Some More Points About Lifting

To review, the term lifting denotes Excel formulas' current multi-result potential, now elevated to a veritable default for most of its functions. But there are few more facts about lifting about which you need to know.

Here's a pair of ranges in C3:D6 (File: *Lifting-Additional Features*) whose values we want to subject to a row-by-row multiplication, as in Figure 3-6.

23	54
45	32
64	45
12	31

Figure 3-6. *Times after times – values to be multiplied*

In E3 we could write

$$=C3:C6*D3:D6$$

And we see in Figure 3-7 that expression results in the following.

23	54	1242	=C3:C6*D3:D6
45	32	1440	
64	45	2880	
12	31	372	

Figure 3-7. *Products of our labors*

We've again encountered an instance of pairwise lifting, that mode of lifting in which pairs of values are multiplied down their columns. Remember that our initial meet-up with pairwise lifting compared student test responses to an answer key, under the steam of an IF statement. Here, we've run through a set of *multiplications* with the pairs.

On the other hand, this sort of lifting need not literally be confined to pairs; it could be stretched across three or more columns of values, once you've made sure you've gotten the syntax right, for example, in Figure 3-8.

23	54	34	42228	=C3:C6*D3:D6*E3:E6
45	32	56	80640	
64	45	43	123840	
12	31	76	28272	

Figure 3-8. *Thrice is nice: multiplying trios of values*

Now that all works. But if we return to our original pairs of values and edit its formula, we'll see that *this* rendition in Figure 3-9 *won't* work, at least not completely.

23	54	1242	=C3:C6*D3:D5
45	32	1440	
64	45	2880	
12	31	#N/A	

Figure 3-9. *An im-paired formula*

You see why. The two ranges don't line up properly – because one bears four cells, the other three. The entry in C6 multiplies itself by a phantom partner, for example, the missing D6, and its formula has no choice but to surrender to an #NA.

Now for a New Angle

But what about this variation, captured in Figure 3-10? Note the new discrepancy: the reference preceding the asterisk comprises four cells, while the one following it offers only three.

23	54	32	45	=C3:C6*D3:F3
45				
64				
12				

Figure 3-10. *Reorienting the formula*

Write that formula in D7 and Figure 3-11 shows you what you'll see as follows.

23	54	32	45	=C3:C6*D3:F3
45				
64				
12				
	1242	736	1035	
	2430	1440	2025	
	3456	2048	2880	
	648	384	540	

Figure 3-11. *... that one works*

Surprise. The second range – which, remember, comprises fewer values than the first one – now stands in a perpendicular relation to the first, and along with that 90-degree shift comes a wholesale rewording of the formula's marching orders. Now, each value in the first range *is multiplied by every value in the second range*. For example, the first value (the upper-left cell) in this brand-new spill – 1242 – is nothing else but the product of the first cells of the respective ranges, 23 and 54. Proceeding horizontally, the 736 signifies the product of 23 x 32, and you can probably take it from there.

What we see here is an instance of what's called *broadcasting,* a property of dynamic arrays by which the resulting set of values assumes the number of rows of the lengthier range, and the number of columns of the *longer* range – here, 4 and 3, respectively. The bottom line is that every permutation is realized – every value is multiplied by every value. But remember, if you need to reference the formula above, all that's required is

=D7#

Of course, broadcasting isn't just specific to multiplication. This formula in Figure 3-12, driven by addition,

23	54	32	45 =C3:C6+D3:F3
45			
64			
12			
	77	55	68
	99	77	90
	118	96	109
	66	44	57

Figure 3-12. *Broadcasting: the addition edition*

works too.

But what about the following (Figure 3-13)?

23	54 =C3:C6*D3
45	
64	
12	

Figure 3-13. *Going it alone: a one-cell broadcast*

Yes, Figure 3-14 shows us that it works.

23	54 =C3:C6*D3
45	
64	
12	
	1242
	2430
	3456
	648

Figure 3-14. *E unum pluribus: out of one (cell), many*

But how does it work? My theory is that Excel treats the single value as a narrowest-possible-*row*, broadcasting it across the four values lining the column.

But terminology aside, you'll want to understand how broadcasting works, because as we'll see, it can work for you.

PMT Permutations

Case in point: For a subtler and more practical lesson, let's see how broadcasting can furnish a series of answers to a question posed by the PMT function. PMT calculates the payments owed on a loan or a mortgage, provided that the user feeds it three bits of information, (1) the loan amount, (2) the number of pay periods spanned by the term of the loan, and (3) the loan's operative interest rate. PMT looks like this:

=PMT(interest rate divided by number of annual payments,number of payments,loan amount)

Thus, for example, if we wanted to learn the required payment for a $10,000 loan (which we'll enter in say, cell A1) at a 3% interest rate (A2) spread across 2 year's worth of monthly payments (in A3 – the number 24), PMT would look like this:

=PMT(A2/12,A3,A1)

To explain it: the interest in A2 must be divided by 12, in order to reflect the number of payments per *year* issued against the 3% rate. A3 simply records the total number of loan payments (12 payments over each of the 2 years, or 24), and the A1 recalls the $10,000 loan sum. The answer: $-429.81, expressed as a negative number simply because the loan debits the borrower's account. As such, the A1 is commonly entered -A1 in order to restore a positive sign to the result; but that decision is merely presentational.

No, we haven't seen any broadcasting yet, but your patience will be rewarded: we want to determine, via a single PMT formula, the sum we'd owe across a *variety* of payment and interest possibilities, represented by matrix you see when you open the *PMT permutations* practice file, and Figure 3-15.

	$ 10,000.00				
	2%	3%	4%	5%	6%
12					
24					
36					
48					
60					
72					

Figure 3-15. *The loan arranger*

(The user would need to enter the row and column values you see – after all, it's the user who decides on the values that would be applied to the loan.) That sure sounds like a job for a dynamic array formula. Here, the loan figure appears in G4, the rates sweep across G7:K7, and the number of prospective payments plunge down F8:F13; and the formula, which we'll write in G8, looks like this:

$$=PMT(G7:K7/12,F8:F13,G4)$$

When the dust settles, we get as follows, per Figure 3-16.

	$ 10,000.00				
	2%	3%	4%	5%	6%
12	-842.39	-846.94	-851.50	-856.07	-860.66
24	-425.40	-429.81	-434.25	-438.71	-443.21
36	-286.43	-290.81	-295.24	-299.71	-304.22
48	-216.95	-221.34	-225.79	-230.29	-234.85
60	-175.28	-179.69	-184.17	-188.71	-193.33
72	-147.50	-151.94	-156.45	-161.05	-165.73

Figure 3-16. *For your interest: a loan payment matrix, courtesy of one dynamic array formula*

Our PMT formula simultaneously inspects every interest rate with the G7:K7/12 argument, and each and every payment frequency via F8:F13. It thus breaks with a conventional PMT by citing *ranges* instead of single cell references – in other words, it's a dynamic array formula. The informative upshot, then, all the payment possibilities unfold before the borrower, thanks to that one dynamic array formula.

And whether you realize it or not, our exercise emulates Excel's ancient Data Table tool, an early array-driven feature with an assortment of moving parts (some of which are rather odd) that, between you and me, I've never quite understood (for a Microsoft tutorial on Data Tables look here (`https://support.microsoft.com/en-us/office/calculate-multiple-results-by-using-a-data-table-e95e2487-6ca6-4413-ad12-77542a5ea50b`)). But never mind; our PMT does the same thing with one formula.

More Lifting – but This Time, Inside a Cell

Now we need to consider one more property of lifting, and it's an important one. Here's the demo example, one we can pursue on a blank worksheet. Every Excel character possesses a code number that's registered by the CODE function. For example, =CODE("b") yields 98, while the upper-case variant =CODE("B") evaluates to 66. Now suppose that, for whatever reason, we need to learn the code of each of the characters in the word Thursday, which we'll enter in cell A6. Our challenge is to write *one* formula that'll do the job, and in order to achieve that end we'll need to somehow separate, or extract, each character from Thursday, so that we can peg the proper code to the proper character.

To embark on our mission we're going to turn to another gray-haired, trusted Excel function – MID. A first cousin of LEFT and RIGHT, MID enables the user to extract text of a specified number of characters from a starting position somewhere *inside* the cell. Thus, this expression

$$=MID(A6,4,2)$$

will trot out the result rs for the word Thursday.

MID's three elements (or "arguments," as they're known in the rule book) (1) name the cell on which MID operates, (2) identify the position number of the character from which MID starts its work, and (3) declare the number of characters to be peeled from the cell. Because it's the r that sits in the fourth position in our Thursday text string, MID commences there and uproots both the r and the s – the 2 characters cited in the last function argument.

But we want something different from MID: we want it to isolate every one of Thursday's eight letters, so that each one can be evaluated by the CODE function. Here's our formula, lodged in A8:

$$=MID(A6,\{1,2,3,4,5,6,7,8\},1)$$

Of course it's the bracketed element that calls for some explanation. Once again we've written an array, one that's positioned as MID's second argument – the one that signals the character location from which to begin extracting characters. Here we're instructing MID to extract one character (referenced by the third function argument – the 1) from the text string's first position, and *then* from its *second* position, and then its third position, and so on, until all eight characters have been skimmed from the source cell. Thus far, then, the formula's spilled results look like this, as portrayed by Figure 3-17.

Thursday							
T	h	u	r	s	d	a	y
=MID(A6,{1,2,3,4,5,6,7,8},1)							

Figure 3-17. *Confined to their cells; MID extracts each character.*

Our MID-based array formula spills its eight results across a horizontal range. MID has in effect applied itself eight times, performing eight character extractions in sequence across its target word, a remarkably nimble feat. And unlike the previous instances of lifting we've surveyed to date, the multi-cell *output* orchestrated here springs from a *single cell*, and that's a capability you very much need to keep in mind, and one we need to reexamine.

Now that we've lifted each character from Thursday into a cell all its own, we can see in Figure 3-18 how the CODE function wraps itself around MID.

Thursday								
84	104	117	114	115	100	97	121	
=CODE(MID(C6,{1,2,3,4,5,6,7,8},1))								

Figure 3-18. *Thursday, Excel style*

Once MID separates the letters, one per cell, the CODE function examines each one and applies its particular code. And all the work has been powered by one formula. That's real dynamic array power. And remember: neither MID nor CODE is a "new" dynamic array function – but they work dynamically, just the same.

Field Notes: Field and Dataset Names

Now that we've battened down our understanding of spills, #s, and the gotta-know essentials of lifting, we can begin to extend a specific welcome to the newest arrivals to the Excel function family – the ones bearing the dynamic array pedigree.

But before we kick off the reviews, a few words about the field and dataset names used here will help clarify the discussions. In the interests of simplicity and training our focus on dynamic arrays, fields will be named after the entries in their header rows unless others indicated. If an exercise requires a reference to the entire dataset, that set will be called All, if it's static – that is, if the data are to remain as you see them, and not receive any new records. All field names in static datasets – including the global All itself – will work with ranges whose coordinates begin with the row immediately *beneath* the headers.

Datasets that *are* prepared to take on new records will have been configured as *tables* via the standard Ctrl-T keyboard sequence, and they'll be named Table1, Table2, etc. – but their fields will again simply *carry the names of their headers*. That latter qualification is necessary, because tables generate default field names exhibiting what Excel calls structured references.

Thus for this table in Figure 3-19,

Country	Salesperson	Order Date	OrderID	Order Amount
France	Buchanan	5/27/2019	10249	£ 2,365.76
Mexico	Peacock	5/27/2019	10250	£ 3,597.90
UK	Peacock	5/29/2019	10251	£ 1,552.60
UK	Dodsworth	5/31/2019	10252	£ 896.35
France	Leverling	6/1/2019	10253	£ 654.06
Mexico	Peacock	6/2/2019	10254	£ 1,444.80
UK	King	6/3/2019	10255	£ 517.80
France	Peacock	6/8/2019	10256	£ 1,119.90
Canada	Davolio	6/9/2019	10257	£ 1,142.03
UK	Callahan	6/11/2019	10258	£ 584.00
Mexico	Leverling	6/11/2019	10259	£ 100.80
France	Peacock	6/15/2019	10260	£ 1,504.65
UK	Peacock	6/16/2019	10261	£ 448.00
UK	Dodsworth	8/7/2019	10262	£ 1,873.80

Figure 3-19. *The table is set*

a standard, by-the-book *table* formula that would count the number of entries in the Salesperson field would read, per Excel's default nomenclature,

=COUNTA(Table1[Salesperson])

But in the interests of consistency and intelligibility, we'll amend the formula to simply read

=COUNTA(Salesperson)

Thus, the above field-name type will appear in *both* kinds of datasets – the static and the table variants.

Thus if you too want, in the interests of following and clicking along, to simplify table field names per the above, do the following *before* you transform the dataset into a table:

- Click anywhere among the data.

- Click Ctrl-A, thus selecting all the dataset cells.

- Then click the Formulas tab > Create from Selection command in the Defined Names button group. You'll see as in Figure 3-20.

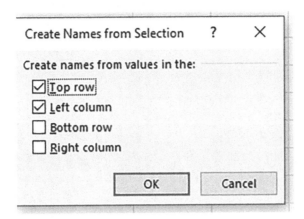

Figure 3-20. *An oldie but goodie: the Create from Selection dialog box*

By clicking OK, this ancient Excel option will proceed to name each field in the dataset after its header (you can also untick the Left column box if you wish).

- *Then* click Ctrl-T to refurbish the dataset into a table.

Now you've gifted yourself with the best of both worlds – you've fashioned a table whose fields will automatically register any new records in a formula, and you've also allowed yourself to work with conventional, header-based field names.

A final point. From here on, in addition to depicting formulas via the FORMULATEXT function, screenshots will color the cells containing formulas yellow, enhancing clarity.

Next Up

Now that we've addressed those necessary preliminaries, it's time to dive deeply into those dynamic array functions. First up: a function we've already glimpsed in passing – SEQUENCE.

CHAPTER 4

The SEQUENCE Function: Made to Order

What's New About Sequence

Of course, Excel has long afforded us the means for unrolling a sequence of values across, or down, a spreadsheet. If you needed to enter a skein of numbers 1 through 100, we'd just enter the 1 and the 2 – thus establishing the desired interval, or step, of 1 – grab onto the AutoFill button, and pull it down 98 more rows, or across for as many columns. Moreover, if you had already entered a list of 100 names, you could post the 1 and 2 in the adjoining left column, select that tandem of values, and double-click the AutoFill button. Presto – 3 through 100 would appear.

But with the advent of the SEQUENCE function, a whole new batch of numbering scenarios has been dropped into your lap, or at least your laptop. Its basic structure isn't too daunting either:

=SEQUENCE(no. of rows,no. of columns,first value,step)

Let's explain by way of a straightforward example. This formula

=SEQUENCE(30,1,1,1)

will elaborate a sequence 30 rows high, one column wide, begin the sequence with the value 1, and step, or increment, each succeeding value by 1. In other words, write the above formula and you wind up with numbers 1 through 30 diving down a column.

But it gets easier. You can omit any of the four arguments, each of which will default to the value 1. Thus

=SEQUENCE(30)

41

© Abbott Ira Katz 2023
A. I. Katz, *Up Up and Array!*, https://doi.org/10.1007/978-1-4842-8966-2_4

will do precisely the same thing as its predecessor above – it will output the values 1 through 30 down a column. And this

=SEQUENCE(,30)

will sequence the 1–30 values *across* a column. But here you do need to enter that initial comma, in order to alert the formula that the 30 has leapfrogged the row argument and bounded into the column reference.

And if you try

=SEQUENCE(30,,6,2)

30 rows' (and one column's) worth of values starting with 6 and stepping up in increments of 2 will result, for example, in 6,8,10,12, etc.

Just a couple more, though you're doubtless getting the idea. Bang out

=SEQUENCE(10,3,,4)

And you'll fashion, as we see in Figure 4-1.

=SEQUENCE(10,3,,4)		
1	5	9
13	17	21
25	29	33
37	41	45
49	53	57
61	65	69
73	77	81
85	89	93
97	101	105
109	113	117

Figure 4-1. *A step-up in columns: three columns, ten rows worth of the sequence*

Note, by the way, that here the sequence spills *across* its rows, and not down.

And if you fire up this expression

=SEQUENCE(12,,,0)

This happens in Figure 4-2.

=SEQUENCE(12,,,0)

1
1
1
1
1
1
1
1
1
1
1
1

Figure 4-2. *At the risk of repeating ourselves*

The 0 step means just that; nothing is added to the next sequenced value. Start with 1 and end up with 1 – 12 times.

And let's remind ourselves that all of these sequences radiate from a single formula. Remember – we're in dynamic array territory.

The Possibilities Proliferate

Now that you're getting the hang of SEQUENCE you can begin to think of all sorts of ways in which the function can do your bidding, sometimes in conjunction with other functions, and with some judicious formatting.

Start with a simple but useful task. You're managing an expanding list of names that you'll like to number automatically, per Figure 4-3 (file: *Numbered List*).

Number	Name
	Emily
	Jack
	Arthur
	Sally

Figure 4-3. *Up for the count: list of names to be numbered*

In cell A2, the one to the immediate left of Emily, we can write

=SEQUENCE(COUNTA(B2:B1000))

By counting the number of names in the B column – currently four – we've in effect written

=SEQUENCE(4)

And that counts off the sequence of values 1 through 4. Enter additional names and the count is correspondingly raised, feeding more numbers to the sequence in Figure 4-4.

Number	Name			
1	Emily	=SEQUENCE(COUNTA(B2:B1000))		
2	Jack			
3	Arthur			
4	Sally			
5	Jane			
6	Xavier			

Figure 4-4. *The A list, numbered in the A column*

Simple but useful indeed, though a couple of cautions need be sounded. For one, don't try to assign IDs to names via this technique, because if you sort the names, the numbers won't follow along with them. The SEQUENCE formula merely counts the names, but has no interest in which name currently finds itself alongside any spilled value. And secondly, remember – you can't write the above formula to a table.

Note   Though we observed earlier that you can't normally delete a spilled value (as opposed to the actual formula), you *can* here delete a row containing one of the values, and the SEQUENCE will recalibrate accordingly. Thus, if you delete the row containing the sequenced value 3, the row beneath will acquire the 3, etc.

Spates of Dates

Now for a variant on a well-known SEQUENCE capability: its talent for spilling a series of consecutive dates down, across, or down *and* across a spill range. For example, this formula

=SEQUENCE(5,7,TODAY(),1)

will elicit a series of dates poured down five rows, pulling across seven columns, anchored by the current date (whenever that is), and incremented by one day, for example, Figure 4-5.

=SEQUENCE(5,7,TODAY(),1)						
4/13/2022	4/14/2022	4/15/2022	4/16/2022	4/17/2022	4/18/2022	4/19/2022
4/20/2022	4/21/2022	4/22/2022	4/23/2022	4/24/2022	4/25/2022	4/26/2022
4/27/2022	4/28/2022	4/29/2022	4/30/2022	5/1/2022	5/2/2022	5/3/2022
5/4/2022	5/5/2022	5/6/2022	5/7/2022	5/8/2022	5/9/2022	5/10/2022
5/11/2022	5/12/2022	5/13/2022	5/14/2022	5/15/2022	5/16/2022	5/17/2022

Figure 4-5. *35 days, one formula*

(The array reflects the Short Date format.) The TODAY function returns the current date, of course, but remember that dates are ultimately numbers, counted off from a baseline of January 1, 1900. Thus 4/13/2022 is "really" 44664 – the number of days separating it from January 1, 1900 – and is regarded as such by our SEQUENCE formula, though of course you're going to format 44664 back into 4/13/2022. Save the workbook in which you've written the formula, open it the next day, and you'll discover that the entire sequence has been ratcheted up by one day. But if you wanted to pin your mini-calendar to an unwavering 4/13/2022 inception point, you'd write

=SEQUENCE(5,7,44664,1)

And treat the spill to the appropriate date format.
You could also write something like

=SEQUENCE(365,,44562)

44562 signifies January 1, 2022, and so our formula will sequence all the days of 2022 down one column – and enable you to enter notes associated with each date in the column to its immediate right. Remember that the omitted arguments here – the column count and the step number – default to 1.

Now what about sequencing times of day? Say we want to portray the 12-hour sequence extending from 6:00 a.m. to 6:00 p.m. down a row. Remember that times are expressed in spreadsheets as fractions of a 24-hour day; thus, noon is rendered as .5

or 1/2, with 10 p.m. evaluating to .916666, or 11/12. Proceeding from that premise, our formula would look like this:

$$=SEQUENCE(13,,6/24,1/24)$$

To break down the formula: the 13 attests to the number of rows required by the sequence – 13, because the first row returns 6:00 a.m., and we need 12 more to mark out the intervals for all 12 hours.

The 6/24, which could have alternatively been written ¼ or .25, puts the start value of the sequence in place – because 6/24, or one-quarter of the day, translates to 6:00 a.m. And the fraction 1/24 issues the step, or increment, that bumps each value in the sequence upwards. 1/24, after all, is spreadsheet language for one hour, and so the sequence spills 6/24, 7/24, 8/24, and so on, until it comes to a halt at 18/24, or 6:00 p.m. Formatted in time terms, we get in Figure 4-6.

=SEQUENCE(13,,6/24,1/24)
6:00:00 AM
7:00:00 AM
8:00:00 AM
9:00:00 AM
10:00:00 AM
11:00:00 AM
12:00:00 PM
1:00:00 PM
2:00:00 PM
3:00:00 PM
4:00:00 PM
5:00:00 PM
6:00:00 PM

Figure 4-6. Dawn to dusk; 12 hours via SEQUENCE

PMT, Again: The Sequel, with Sequence

Now that you've honed your SEQUENCE chops, let's make our way back to the PMT exercise we stepped through last chapter, in which we let loose a dynamic array formula across a flurry of loan interest/payment-period possibilities in Figure 4-7.

	$ 10,000.00				
	2%	3%	4%	5%	6%
12	-842.39	-846.94	-851.50	-856.07	-860.66
24	-425.40	-429.81	-434.25	-438.71	-443.21
36	-286.43	-290.81	-295.24	-299.71	-304.22
48	-216.95	-221.34	-225.79	-230.29	-234.85
60	-175.28	-179.69	-184.17	-188.71	-193.33
72	-147.50	-151.94	-156.45	-161.05	-165.73

Figure 4-7. *Take two: the PMT formula, about to be teamed with SEQUENCE*

There, the interest rates and payment frequencies bordering the PMT outcomes were simply *typed*; but now that we're clued in about SEQUENCE, why can't the rates holding down G7:K7 be made to unfold this way, if we squirrel our formula into G7?

=SEQUENCE(,5,0.02,0.01)

Five columns, a start number of .02 (2%, of course, in the desired formatting), and an interval of .01.

And we could be similarly inspired about the payment-frequency range pushing down F8:F13, to write in F8:

=SEQUENCE(6,,12,12)

And those expressions prompt a rewrite of the actual PMT formula in G8 as illustrated by Figure 4-8.

=PMT(G7#/12,F8#,G4)

		$ 10,000.00				
		=SEQUENCE(,5,0.02,0.01)				
		2%	3%	4%	5%	6%
=SEQUENCE(6,,12,12)	12	-842.39	-846.94	-851.50	-856.07	-860.66
	24	-425.40	-429.81	-434.25	-438.71	-443.21
	36	-286.43	-290.81	-295.24	-299.71	-304.22
	48	-216.95	-221.34	-225.79	-230.29	-234.85
	60	-175.28	-179.69	-184.17	-188.71	-193.33
	72	-147.50	-151.94	-156.45	-161.05	-165.73
		=PMT(G7#/12,F8#,G4)				

Figure 4-8. *Three formulas, 30 rates*

(And note the pound-sign references in the formula.)

Our results here reproduce those we achieved through conventional means in Chapter 3, and so they beg the obvious question: why bother? The answer is that now we can cycle through many more payment possibilities, by simply editing the formulas. For example, replace the 5 with an 8 in the interest rate SEQUENCE, as in Figure 4-9.

		$ 10,000.00							
		=SEQUENCE(,8,0.02,0.01)							
		2%	3%	4%	5%	6%	7%	8%	9%
=SEQUENCE(6,,12,12)	12	-842.39	-846.94	-851.50	-856.07	-860.66	-865.27	-869.88	-874.51
	24	-425.40	-429.81	-434.25	-438.71	-443.21	-447.73	-452.27	-456.85
	36	-286.43	-290.81	-295.24	-299.71	-304.22	-308.77	-313.36	-318.00
	48	-216.95	-221.34	-225.79	-230.29	-234.85	-239.46	-244.13	-248.85
	60	-175.28	-179.69	-184.17	-188.71	-193.33	-198.01	-202.76	-207.58
	72	-147.50	-151.94	-156.45	-161.05	-165.73	-170.49	-175.33	-180.26
		=PMT(G7#/12,F8#,G4)							

Figure 4-9. *Compounding our interest: 48 payment plans*

And for an even more efficient workaround, you could write, for example,

=SEQUENCE(,G1,0.02,0.01)

which would enable you to enter any value in G1 without having to edit the formula. The G1 entry would record as many interest intervals as you require.

And of course, you can do much the same for the payment frequencies, by substituting a new value for the 6 in its SEQUENCE. Thus we see that by working dynamically, new scenarios can suggest themselves in a flash.

The One-Formula Multiplication Table

Now let's move from time to times. Suppose we want to construct a multiplication table – not of the old-school kind (literally), but rather a *dynamic* table, one that can grab any two ranges of values and flash all their multiplied products immediately. SEQUENCE can do the job – and with a grand total of one formula.

Start with a blank worksheet and enter the numbers 5 in B6 and 10 in C6. Those entries will impart, on our first go-round, the values 1 through 5 down a column and 1 through 10 across a set of columns, helping to form the outline of a matrix that will multiply every value by every other one.

Now here comes the formula. Enter, in C9,

$$=SEQUENCE(B6)*SEQUENCE(,C6)$$

And as we see in Figure 4-10.

5	10								
=SEQUENCE(B6)*SEQUENCE(,C6)									
1	2	3	4	5	6	7	8	9	10
2	4	6	8	10	12	14	16	18	20
3	6	9	12	15	18	21	24	27	30
4	8	12	16	20	24	28	32	36	40
5	10	15	20	25	30	35	40	45	50

Figure 4-10. *The times they are a-changin': a one-formula dynamic multiplication table*

Cool, if I do say so myself. Now enter different values in B6 and C6, and the table changes to reflect the new inputs, with the number of columns and rows expanding and contracting accordingly. It's dynamic.

In fact, this formula takes us back to a lesson we've already learned, that is, our discussion in Chapter 3 of how perpendicular ranges behave toward one another. There we noted that if we multiply two such ranges, each value in the first range is multiplied by every value in the second – and that's exactly what's happening here. The first SEQUENCE formula dispatches its values down a column, and the second pushes its values across, at a right angle to the first. The difference here is that the two SEQUENCE formulas haven't scooped up their values from ranges in the worksheet, as they did in Chapter 3; the 1-5 and 1-10 sequences have been assembled *inside their formulas,* after which all the results spill onto the matrix.

Rewriting the CODE

We'll close our look at SEQUENCE with another follow-up to Chapter 3, an important addendum to the discussion there of the array we wrote inside MID, that in turn nested itself inside the CODE function, recalled in Figure 4-11.

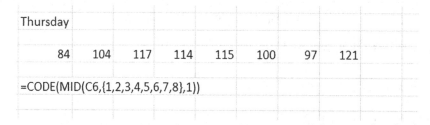

Thursday							
84	104	117	114	115	100	97	121
=CODE(MID(C6,{1,2,3,4,5,6,7,8},1))							

Figure 4-11.   *The array inside MID, inside CODE*

There, we hard-coded, or typed, the bracketed array surrounding values 1 through 8, each standing for the position of a letter in the word Thursday. Now let's try this revised version:

=CODE(MID(C6,SEQUENCE(LEN(C6)),1))

This formula works, too. SEQUENCE(LEN(C6)) has substituted itself for the brackets in the first edition of the formula, here measuring the *length* of the word Thursday in C6 – eight characters. In effect, then, we've written

=SEQUENCE(8)

which of course sequences to 1,2,3,4,5,6,7,8, emulating the bracketed activity in Chapter 3; and those eight values again extract the word's eight characters, after which the CODE function identifies the code of each. But SEQUENCE is far more efficient, because if we enter a *different* word in C6 of any length, SEQUENCE(LEN(C6)) will count its characters, too, and deliver the count to CODE, for example, Figure 4-12.

dumbwaiter	
100	=CODE(MID(C6,SEQUENCE(LEN(C6)),1))
117	
109	
98	
119	
97	
105	
116	
101	
114	

Figure 4-12. *Ten characters to count? No problem*

And that's clearly the more effective and powerful approach.

But of course, you've noticed a discrepancy: unlike the horizontal output of the codes we engineered in Chapter 3, the formula here piles the results *vertically*. The reason: again, SEQUENCE(LEN(C6)) offers the functional equivalent of SEQUENCE(10), the number of characters populating the word dumbwaiter. But SEQUENCE(10), as we've learned, only makes use of SEQUENCE's *first* argument – thus registering the number of *rows* to be spilled. If we want our spill to scoot across the *columns* as it did in Chapter 3, we write instead

=CODE(MID(C6,SEQUENCE(,LEN(C6)),1))

That little comma preceding LEN pushes LEN(C6) into SEQUENCE's *second* argument, where it moves into column territory.

Looking Ahead

But I do go on. You've doubtless gotten the point of SEQUENCE by now, and with just a few practice go-rounds you'll be a SEQUENCE savant. Now we can pay a visit to another member of the dynamic array crew – UNIQUE.

CHAPTER 5

UNIQUE: A Singular Function

What's Unique About It?

The UNIQUE dynamic array function hurdles an old spreadsheet stumbling block – how to extract a unique set of entries from a field – without breaking a sweat. For example, we might need to compile a list of the salespersons archived in the Salesperson field of this dataset (file: *UNIQUE*), as portrayed in Figure 5-1.

Country	Salesperson	Order Date	OrderID	Order Amount
France	Buchanan	5/27/2019	10249	£ 2,365.76
Mexico	Peacock	5/27/2019	10250	£ 3,597.90
UK	Peacock	5/29/2019	10251	£ 1,552.60
UK	Dodsworth	5/31/2019	10252	£ 896.35
France	Leverling	6/1/2019	10253	£ 654.06
Mexico	Peacock	6/2/2019	10254	£ 1,444.80
UK	King	6/3/2019	10255	£ 517.80
France	Peacock	6/8/2019	10256	£ 1,119.90
Canada	Davolio	6/9/2019	10257	£ 1,142.03
UK	Callahan	6/11/2019	10258	£ 584.00
Mexico	Leverling	6/11/2019	10259	£ 100.80
France	Peacock	6/15/2019	10260	£ 1,504.65
UK	Peacock	6/16/2019	10261	£ 448.00
UK	Dodsworth	8/7/2019	10262	£ 1,873.80
Canada	Leverling	6/17/2019	10263	£ 346.56

Figure 5-1. *Selling point: Salesperson data to be subject to the UNIQUE function*

The problem, of course, is the recurring appearances of each salesperson's name in the field – because we want to view each name exactly once.

© Abbott Ira Katz 2023
A. I. Katz, *Up Up and Array!*, https://doi.org/10.1007/978-1-4842-8966-2_5

And that demand sends out a casting call for UNIQUE, which makes its debut with a simple formula:

=UNIQUE(Salesperson)

And that formula merits rave reviews for staging this result now playing in Figure 5-2.

=UNIQUE(Salesperson)
Buchanan
Peacock
Dodsworth
Leverling
King
Davolio
Callahan
Suyama
Fuller

Figure 5-2. *One time only: each salesperson listed uniquely*

Bravo – Excel users have been looking for that kind of performance for a long time.

And if you redefine the dataset as a table and introduce new names to the Salesperson field, UNIQUE will see to it that their names will automatically appear in its result.

And of course, UNIQUE can be mixed and matched with other functions, for example,

=COUNTA(UNIQUE(Salesperson))

which will yield 9. And

=SORT(UNIQUE(Salesperson))

will again return the salesperson names uniquely, but this time in alphabetical order (SORT and SORTBY will make their official appearance in the next chapter).

How It Works

The above formulas read pretty self-evidently, confirming what is surely UNIQUE's primary use, for example, prospecting unique values in a particular field. But the function has a couple of additional, optional arguments that you'll want to know about, even though you're far less likely to put them into play:

=UNIQUE(range/array,by column,exactly once)

Note The "range/array" term simply identifies the data to be impacted by the function, recognizing that, as a terminological matter, one person's range may be another's array. Here, range and array are in effect equivalent.

We've already applied the range argument above (Excel officially terms the range argument "array," but we're tiptoeing past that definitional morass, as we will with other functions), and it requires little in the way of elaboration. If you want to distill the unique entries in a range, just enter UNIQUE, open a parenthesis, and enter a range name or its coordinates. The optional by column argument enables the user to identify unique elements in a *horizontal* range. Thus if B7:F7 looks like Figure 5-3,

Jane	Ted	Mark	Ted	Alice

Figure 5-3. *Getting re-oriented; finding unique names in a horizontal range*

the formula

=UNIQUE(B7:F7,1)

will realize in Figure 5-4.

=UNIQUE(B7:F7,1)			
Jane	Ted	Mark	Alice

Figure 5-4. *Something's missing: only unique names returned*

Note that, unlike SEQUENCE, both vertical and horizontal ranges are referenced by UNIQUE in the *first* argument. It's the optional 1 that orders the formula to recognize the range as a horizontal one (you can also enter the word TRUE in lieu of the value 1).

UNIQUE's third, optional argument is a bit quirky. It ferrets only those entries in a range that appear exactly one time. Thus, writing

=UNIQUE(B7:F7,1,1)

will yield Jane, Mark, Alice (again the 1 associated with the third argument can also be replaced by the term TRUE).

While you may be hard-pressed to dream up a real-world use for the exactly once alternative, here's a couple of possibilities. If you needed to search a list of names for typos, the exactly once option could – could – be of some service. If you had mistakenly keyed in Peacock once in the Salesperson field, UNIQUE's third argument would find it – but of course if I had committed the same error multiple times, it would not.

You could also apply the exactly once argument to, say, a list of student names in which each name is to be entered a solitary time. Running UNIQUE with the exactly once argument would then simply duplicate the entire list – but would *exclude* any name inadvertently entered twice.

UNIQUE Stretching Across Multiple Fields

What if you want to extricate unique instances of data across two or more fields? For example, I want to learn the countries in which each salesperson does business, that is, I want each salesperson to be listed alongside each country in which he/she conducts sales once each. We can mobilize that outcome via this formula:

=UNIQUE(Country:Salesperson)

Resulting in (in excerpt) Figure 5-5.

=UNIQUE(Country:Salesperson)

France	Buchanan
Mexico	Peacock
UK	Peacock
UK	Dodsworth
France	Leverling
UK	King
France	Peacock
Canada	Davolio
UK	Callahan
Mexico	Leverling
Canada	Leverling
France	Callahan
UK	Davolio
UK	Suyama

Figure 5.5. *Internationally unique: each salesperson is matched to every country in which he/she works*

(Again, these data can be sorted, and you'd probably want to do just that; but the how-to's of sorting will be reserved for the next chapter.)

The formula works by deploying the semicolon to link the adjoining Country and Salespersons fields, building a kind of meta-field which, understood in cell reference terms, reads A2:B799. And UNIQUE then proceeds to dispatch every unique *combination* of Country and Salesperson to the spill range.

And if you sought unique permutations across three adjacent fields, you'd write

=UNIQUE(first field:third field)

That expression would span the three fields.

Distant Fields

But what if the fields contributing to your UNIQUE search aren't neighboring one another? What if, for example, Country and Salesperson were separated by a third field that doesn't figure in your plans, for example (File: *UNIQUE,* the *Non-adjacent UNIQUE* worksheet), in Figure 5-6?

Country	Order Date	Salesperson	OrderID	Order Amount
France	5/27/2019	Buchanan	10249	£ 2,365.76
Mexico	5/27/2019	Peacock	10250	£ 3,597.90
UK	5/29/2019	Peacock	10251	£ 1,552.60
UK	5/31/2019	Dodsworth	10252	£ 896.35
France	6/1/2019	Leverling	10253	£ 654.06
Mexico	6/2/2019	Peacock	10254	£ 1,444.80
UK	6/3/2019	King	10255	£ 517.80
France	6/8/2019	Peacock	10256	£ 1,119.90
Canada	6/9/2019	Davolio	10257	£ 1,142.03
UK	6/11/2019	Callahan	10258	£ 584.00
Mexico	6/11/2019	Leverling	10259	£ 100.80
France	6/15/2019	Peacock	10260	£ 1,504.65
UK	6/16/2019	Peacock	10261	£ 448.00
UK	8/7/2019	Dodsworth	10262	£ 1,873.80

Figure 5-6. *Faraway countries: the Country and Salespersons fields are separated by a third field*

Given that scenario, the footwork for gleaning UNIQUEs for Country and Salesperson gets a little fancier. We need to lace on the INDEX function, a classic spreadsheet tool that, like so many other entrenched functions, has undergone a major dynamic-array renovation.

INDEX has traditionally pinpointed a particular cell stationed at the crossroads of a particular row and column. Retrieving the assortment of student grades we introduced in Chapter 2, the ones fanning out across A1:G11 and retrieved by Figure 5-7.

name	soc	phil	poli sci	art	physics	chem
Bill	75	90	89	72	89	79
Dana	55	68	87	47	56	50
Ed	61	38	46	36	88	66
Jack	34	80	81	56	57	64
Jane	66	83	30	72	66	56
Hortense	41	85	53	75	90	45
Paul	71	59	69	61	100	72
Ted	66	66	70	35	76	91
Ulysses	59	52	100	94	38	31
Wanda	84	97	35	52	75	86

Figure 5-7. *Those grades, again*

This INDEX formula

=INDEX(A1:G11,3,4)

would alight on 87, the grade residing in the range's third row and fourth column. But now INDEX has been invested with a new aptitude, an important one – for marking and carving out *whole ranges*. And here, in our case of the Country and Salesperson fields distanced from one another by a third, intervening field, we want INDEX to wrench Country and Salesperson from their current columns and set them down in a new, impromptu dataset consisting of just those two columns/fields; and once they've been reunited, we can run a UNIQUE with the Country:Salesperson pairing we've already seen.

And how do we do that? We write something like this, for starters:

=INDEX(A1:C800,SEQUENCE(ROWS(A1:C800)),{1,3})

And then we wrap UNIQUE around it all.

Now obviously that formula calls for some explaining, even as it reaches back to some familiar elements (remember that we're now working with the dataset filling the *second, Non-adjacent UNIQUE* sheet).

First, the A1:C800 recognizes our need for nothing but the first and third columns in the range, stationed in A and C – the columns storing Country and Salesperson data. We aren't interested in the data in columns D and E, and as such we can exclude them from the initial range reference. But we also need to exclude column B, the field recording the Order Dates – because failing to eject the data in B will result in a UNIQUE that delivers the unique combinations of all *three* columns – A, B, and C.

Second, the SEQUENCE function parallels its role in the MID formula in Chapter 3, in which we searched for the CODE attaching to each letter of a word. Here SEQUENCE partners with ROWS – a function that simply counts the number of rows in a range, in our case 800, and thus in effect yields SEQUENCE(800), which in turn evaluates to 1,2,3,4,...800. *Each* of those values populates the INDEX formula, so that, true to its dynamic array character, each row in the range will be returned by the result. Had we simply written

=INDEX(A1:C800,800,{1,3}))

then *only* row 800 would have been returned.

And as for the bracketed array reference posted to INDEX's column argument, that entry is familiar too; here it selects the first and third columns in the range – the ones featuring the data we want.

And once all those nuts and bolts are screwed into place, you're ready for the finished product:

=UNIQUE(INDEX(A1:C800,SEQUENCE(ROWS(A1:C800)),{1,3}))

And that expression should bring about precisely the same outcomes we see in Figure 5.5.

Note   An alternative to the above exercise will be offered in the chapter on the brand new CHOOSECOLS function.

It's Starting to Add Up

UNIQUE's penchant for grabbing single instances of values or text in a range can be put to highly efficient use to aggregate data by a variable, or variables. To exemplify that abstract pronouncement with a real-world case, suppose we simply want to determine how much money each salesperson earned (we're returning to the first sheet in the *UNIQUE* file). Is that something a pivot table can do? Yep, but the dynamic duo of UNIQUE and the old-school SUMIF (or SUMIFS) can craft a result that can immediately recalculate new data, as well as incorporate new records added to the source data.

To demonstrate, enter =UNIQUE(Salesperson) in cell G4. Then enter in H4

=SUMIF(Salesperson,G4#,Order_Amount)

And the sales totals gather alongside each salesperson, as in Figure 5-8.

=UNIQUE(Salesperson)	Buchanan	70161.39	=SUMIF(Salesperson,G4#,Order_Amount)
	Peacock	227107.68	
	Dodsworth	73453.89	
	Leverling	199334.47	
	King	114247.99	
	Davolio	182027.24	
	Callahan	126586.47	
	Suyama	70664.23	
	Fuller	162503.78	

Figure 5-8. *Selling point: UNIQUE supplies the criteria for SUMIF*

Note the G4# denoting the cell in which UNIQUE is emplaced, and which serves as the SUMIF criterion.

Now what if we wanted to go further and calculate salesperson earnings by country? With that refinement in mind, delete the SUMIF formula in H4, click in H3, and enter

=TRANSPOSE(UNIQUE(Country))

TRANSPOSE is another of Excel's primeval functions that's enjoyed a dramatic upgrade in ease of use. TRANSPOSE shifts the orientation of a range from horizontal to vertical and vice versa, and here it collaborates with UNIQUE to flip the Country results sideways, so to speak demonstrated by Figure 5-9.

		=TRANSPOSE(UNIQUE(Country))			
		France	Mexico	UK	Canada
=UNIQUE(Salesperson)	Buchanan				
	Peacock				
	Dodsworth				
	Leverling				
	King				
	Davolio				
	Callahan				
	Suyama				
	Fuller				

Figure 5-9. *Matrix in the making: Salesperson and Country in a pivot table impression*

Now let's move back into H4 and write

=SUMIFS(Order_Amount,Salesperson,G4#,Country,H3#)

A first cousin of SUMIF, SUMIFS affords the user multiple criteria by which to sum values. Here we've recruited both Salesperson and Country as criteria, denoting both with the dynamic array pound-sign reference. As a result, we get the following, in Figure 5-10.

		=TRANSPOSE(UNIQUE(Country))				
		France	Mexico	UK	Canada	
=UNIQUE(Salesperson)	Buchanan	27161.35	12059.54	20041.65	10898.85	=SUMIFS(Order_Amount,Salesperson,G4#,Country,H3#)
	Peacock	45074.69	44408.35	87023.42	50601.22	
	Dodsworth	7937.91	14506.10	31785.83	19224.05	
	Leverling	18204.67	33413.55	112328.90	35387.35	
	King	21769.16	16276.64	47067.25	29134.94	
	Davolio	20043.41	62376.79	62463.02	37144.02	
	Callahan	33009.52	22670.91	39048.71	31857.33	
	Suyama	19051.41	10172.18	28401.99	13038.65	
	Fuller	30941.38	26320.21	68759.40	36482.79	

Figure 5-10. *Having a field day: Sales totals by the Salesperson and Country fields*

And again, any new Salesperson and/or Country names we add to the dataset will find their places in the above results, once we remake the dataset into a table. But because our formula references the Salesperson and Country in dynamic array terms, no formula rewrite would be necessary.

And yes, the above shot bears a striking resemblance to a pivot table; and indeed, dynamic arrays *can* recreate the number-crunching might of the tables, at least in part (though not completely), and with the advantage of immediately recalculating any new records written to the source data. And that leaves you with one more spreadsheet design decision to make: dynamic arrays or pivot table? Something new to think about.

Up Next

Now that we've concluded our introduction to the UNIQUE function, we can move on to a pair of related dynamic array functions you'll definitely want to learn and master – SORT and SORTBY.

CHAPTER 6

SORT and SORTBY: The ABCs (and the CBAs)

Sorting is one of those go-to spreadsheet ingredients that get tossed into data concoctions all the time. And the tossing has gotten easier across the generations, too. You may not remember the Paleotlithic sorts availing in the early generations of Lotus 1-2-3, in which users had to select the entire dataset to be sorted before going ahead; but then again, you don't have to.

But you'll certainly want to learn, and remember, the new dynamic array takes on sorting promoted by a pair of functions, SORT and SORTBY. What's new about them for starters is that, unlike the traditional sorting regimen we've come to know and use if not love, SORT and SORTBY *don't* sort a database directly. Until now, of course, if you wanted to execute a garden-variety dataset sort by one field, you'd click any cell in the field and then call upon one of the Sort buttons plonked in either the Home or Data ribbon, or one nailed into a right-click-driven context menu. The point again is that, per these techniques, the actual dataset is what gets sorted.

But SORT and SORTBY fabricate a *replica* of the dataset and sort it instead, thus leaving the original data intact. Whether you find that act of duplication a touch messy – because you've in effect made a copy of the original dataset – is your call, and is tied to whatever purposes you've brought to your task. But you'll probably conclude that, for most of your spreadsheet intentions, sorting with SORT and SORTBY is a productive move indeed.

How SORT Works

Like so many Excel functions SORT features several arguments, some of which are optional and ignorable if your sort proceeds along standard lines. It looks like this:

© Abbott Ira Katz 2023
A. I. Katz, *Up Up and Array!*, https://doi.org/10.1007/978-1-4842-8966-2_6

=SORT(range/array,sort_index,sort_order,by_col)

The first argument (which again Excel officially terms "array") simply asks the user to enter the range to be sorted. The sort index asks for the *number* of the column by which the sort is to be conducted, and points to SORT's *default* incapacity to sort by more than one column (more about this later). Thus, if we want to sort this dataset by its Salesperson field realized in Figure 6-1 (file: *SORT*),

Country	Salesperson	Order Date	OrderID	Order Amount
France	Buchanan	5/27/2019	10249	£ 2,365.76
Mexico	Peacock	5/27/2019	10250	£ 3,597.90
UK	Peacock	5/29/2019	10251	£ 1,552.60
UK	Dodsworth	5/31/2019	10252	£ 896.35
France	Leverling	6/1/2019	10253	£ 654.06
Mexico	Peacock	6/2/2019	10254	£ 1,444.80
UK	King	6/3/2019	10255	£ 517.80
France	Peacock	6/8/2019	10256	£ 1,119.90
Canada	Davolio	6/9/2019	10257	£ 1,142.03
UK	Callahan	6/11/2019	10258	£ 584.00
Mexico	Leverling	6/11/2019	10259	£ 100.80
France	Peacock	6/15/2019	10260	£ 1,504.65
UK	Peacock	6/16/2019	10261	£ 448.00
UK	Dodsworth	8/7/2019	10262	£ 1,873.80
Canada	Leverling	6/17/2019	10263	£ 346.56

Figure 6-1. *Salespersons are out of sorts, for the moment*

we'd write

=SORT(All,2)

And befitting its dynamic array character, the formula spills the dataset records, with the salespersons duly ordered as we see in Figure 6-2 (the screen shots here display excerpts of the entire dataset).

=SORT(all,2)				
France	Buchanan	43612.00	10249	2365.76
France	Buchanan	43642.00	10268	642.2
France	Buchanan	43671.00	10294	210
Mexico	Buchanan	43674.00	10304	1420
Canada	Buchanan	43712.00	10337	516
UK	Buchanan	43719.00	10344	877.2
France	Buchanan	43751.00	10366	3471.68
France	Buchanan	43752.00	10367	429.4
France	Buchanan	43764.00	10379	9210.9
Mexico	Buchanan	43774.00	10390	103.2
UK	Buchanan	43788.00	10403	716.72
UK	Buchanan	43852.00	10470	713.3
UK	Buchanan	43867.00	10485	1249.1
Canada	Buchanan	43871.00	10490	558
Mexico	Buchanan	43916.00	10534	946

Figure 6-2. *Buchanan is first among salespersons*

You've doubtless noticed a number of discrepancies between the spilled results and the original source dataset. For one, the data have reverted to their default formats, for example, the Order Dates have been returned to their native numerical format, and Order Amounts display variable decimal point counts. As such, you'd need to restore the desired formats.

Secondly, the sort has disregarded the dataset's field headers, in our case because the All dataset range begins with row 2 (a point we made a few chapters ago). Thus if you need those headers – and you might, of course – you could copy and paste the original atop the spilled results.

Note   Even if your range definition of All includes row 1 – the header row – SORT will continue to ignore it.

Note in addition that if we simply write

$$=SORT(All)$$

the dataset will automatically sort itself by its *first* column. It has to select a column by which to sort, and it opts by default for column/field one.

SORT's third argument, sort order, wants to know if you want to sort the designated ascendingly (by entering a 1) or descendingly (via a -1). But we've already seen that by omitting the argument, the formula executes a default *ascending* sort.

The function's final argument – by column – is perhaps the trickiest, because we're not accustomed to thinking about sorts that order datasets *horizontally*. But SORT nevertheless can do just that.

To illustrate – here's a mini-dataset (named scores) recording the test scores of two students in Figure 6-3 (file: *SORT*, the *SORT by column sheet*).

Test	1	2	3	4
Jane	67	82	61	88
Ted	45	76	72	90

Figure 6-3. *Lateral thinking: sorting by columns*

(Note that the field names here – Test, Jane, and Ted – subsume their data *horizontally*.)

If we want to sort Jane's scores in ascending order we'd write

$$=SORT(scores,3,,1)$$

And Figure 6-4 illustrates what we'd see.

=SORT(scores,3,,1)			
1	3	2	4
67	61	82	88
45	72	76	90

Figure 6-4. *Upward trajectory: Ted's scores, sorted lowest to highest*

Here the 3 in SORT instructs the formula to sort the dataset by its 3rd *row,* the one containing Ted's scores. Again, the field headers have been exempted from the sort.

And of course, SORT can wrap itself around other functions, contributing to productive formula multi-tasking, for example,

=SORT(UNIQUE(Salesperson))

Sorting by Multiple Fields

You'll recall that SORT restricts itself by default to sorting a dataset by one column only. In fact, however, you can tinker with the function to induce it to sort by several fields, via an old friend, or nemesis – the good old, bracketed array constant (thanks to the Ablebits site for this pointer).

If, for example, we want to sort the sales data by Salesperson and *then* by Country, we could write

=SORT(All,{2,1})

Look familiar? Here the array constants denote the second and then the first columns to be sorted respectively by their default ascending order, yielding in Figure 6-5.

=SORT(all,{2,1})				
Canada	Buchanan	43712	10337	516
Canada	Buchanan	43871	10490	558
Canada	Buchanan	44028	10653	1434
Canada	Buchanan	44039	10664	372.37
Canada	Buchanan	44053	10681	1423
Canada	Buchanan	44089	10721	4451.7
Canada	Buchanan	44105	10739	484.25
Canada	Buchanan	44231	10956	1659.53
France	Buchanan	43612	10249	2365.76
France	Buchanan	43642	10268	642.2
France	Buchanan	43671	10294	210
France	Buchanan	43751	10366	3471.68
France	Buchanan	43752	10367	429.4
France	Buchanan	43764	10379	9210.9
France	Buchanan	43979	10598	890

Figure 6-5. *Two-column sort: salespersons first, then countries*

Again, Buchanan tops the Salesperson field, with his/her complement of countries headed by Canada, followed in the sort by France (remember again that a reformatting of the fields may be required).

And what if we wanted to sort by Salesperson name and then by Order Amounts in descending order? That is, we want each salesperson's largest sales hoisted to the top of that field's sort. The formula would look like this:

=SORT(All,{2,5},{1,-1})

Yes, we've trotted out two sets of array constants here – the first, calling for a sort by the second (Salesperson) field and then the fifth (Order Amount), the second requesting that Salesperson be sorted A to Z, and Order Amount Z to A (or highest to lowest). Get that right and you'll see in Figure 6-6.

=SORT(all,{2,5},{1,-1})				
France	Buchanan	43764	10379	9210.9
UK	Buchanan	43993	10612	6475.4
France	Buchanan	44181	10848	4581
Canada	Buchanan	44089	10721	4451.7
Mexico	Buchanan	43937	10554	3554.27
France	Buchanan	43751	10366	3471.68
Mexico	Buchanan	44165	10820	2826
UK	Buchanan	44185	10857	2603
France	Buchanan	43612	10249	2365.76
France	Buchanan	44087	10719	2205.75
UK	Buchanan	43968	10583	2147.4
France	Buchanan	44192	10871	2058.46
Mexico	Buchanan	44033	10658	1779.2
UK	Buchanan	44164	10818	1692.8
Canada	Buchanan	44231	10956	1659.53

Figure 6-6. *Ups and downs: Salesperson sorted A to Z, Order Amount highest to lowest*

Note that by being sorted highest to lowest, Buchanan's order amounts diminish as they trail down the column. By way of corroboration, if we scroll down the results to the next salesperson, Callahan, we'll see in Figure 6-7.

UK	Callahan	44069	10700	4825
UK	Callahan	44242	10977	4813.5
France	Callahan	44182	10852	3812.7
Mexico	Callahan	43703	10326	3741.3
Canada	Callahan	43673	10298	3740
UK	Callahan	44234	10961	3584
Mexico	Callahan	44265	11033	3232.8
Canada	Callahan	43663	10285	3016
UK	Callahan	44182	10853	2984
France	Callahan	44248	10988	2772
UK	Callahan	43796	10413	2713.5
Canada	Callahan	43849	10463	2684
Canada	Callahan	44255	11010	2633.9
Canada	Callahan	43764	10380	2390.4
France	Callahan	44252	11001	2233
UK	Callahan	43929	10546	2222.2

Figure 6-7. More of the same: Callahan comes next in the alphabet with the sales again pointing downward, per a descending sort

Sorting Digits: All in the Same Cell

Our look in Chapter 3 at the dynamic array property of lifting – a formula's skill at performing repeated operations on a set of values – took us to an exercise in which the MID function went about extracting the letters from the word Thursday. Now we want to tap MID on the shoulder again and ask it, in combination with SORT, to numerically order a set of digits (file: *SORT digits*) addressed in cell B4:

1587078421

In other words, we want to end up with

0112457788

And we want those digits recombined into that sequence by a single formula.

The first step, one that recalls the previous exercise, is to extract each digit from the cell, via

=MID(B4,SEQUENCE(LEN(B4)),1)

written in D9 (or any cell of your choosing). Now in fact that formula represents something of an update of the Thursday character extraction, because we've learned in the interim (in Chapter 4) about the SEQUENCE function (see the CODE exercise there), and its ability here to stock the formula with an array of numbers – each of which will supply a character position at which MID will start extracting characters. Thus the SEQUENCE argument above measures the length of 15870708421, in effect declaring

=MID(B4,{1;2;3;4;5;6;7;8;9;10},1)

As a result, Figure 6-8 reveals what we get in D9:

=MID(B4,SEQUENCE(LEN(B4)),1)
1
5
8
7
0
7
8
4
2
1

Figure 6-8. *MIDway through the process: MID extracts each digit*

(Note that the digits are aligned left, hinting that these outputs are actually text, not numerics.)

Now that each digit has been culled from B4 and temporarily housed in a cell all its own, we can surround the MID expression with SORT:

=SORT(MID(B4,SEQUENCE(LEN(B4)),1))

yielding as follows, in Figure 6-9.

=SORT(MID(B4,SEQUENCE(LEN(B4)),1))
0
1
1
2
4
5
7
7
8
8

Figure 6-9. *Neat and tidy spill: the digits, now sorted*

(Again, the digits have inherited a text format, but Excel reads them as quasi-numeric and is able to sort them.)

We're almost there. All that remains to do is embrace the formula with the CONCAT function which combines, or concatenates, text that's been distributed across individual cells:

=CONCAT(SORT(MID(B4,SEQUENCE(LEN(B4)),1)))

We see as follows, per Figure 6-10.

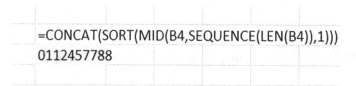

=CONCAT(SORT(MID(B4,SEQUENCE(LEN(B4)),1)))
0112457788

Figure 6-10. *Size places – the digits are sorted*

And of course, any other collection of digits you enter in B4 will be immediately sorted, too.

SORTBY: SORT's Field Correspondent

We've seen that SORT is a highly effective and nimble means for sorting data dynamically; so what then, can SORTBY do that its companion can't?

Let's see. SORTBY's syntax looks like this:

=SORTBY(range/array,**by**_range/array,sort_order,by_range/array2,sort_order...)

Thus, SORTBY enables multi-column sorts – but so does SORT. Moreover, SORTBY *can't* sort a range in a stand-alone, default state, for example,

=SORTBY(All)

And SORT can. So what, then, does SORTBY bring to the party?

Here's what. SORTBY lets the user sort a field, or fields, by another field that *need not appear in the sort result, and need not appear in the same dataset.*

For an example, let's tick the SORTBY sheet in the *SORT* file. I want to sort the names of students in the Name field by their scores in the Art exam – but I want to restrict the actual output to the student names alone. Thus, if we write

=SORTBY(Name,Art,-1)

we get the following, in Figure 6-11.

=SORTBY(name,art,-1)
Clothilde
Vincenza
Maureen
Haseem
Paolo
Agnieska
Hiran
Said
Chen
Ted

Figure 6-11. Pretty picture: Clothilde tops the Art exam scores

Here, SORTBY relies on a sort-by field that's been excluded from the result. (Remember that the -1 argument triggers a descending, highest-to-lowest sort.)

To drive the point home more emphatically, note the eng field that's been severed from the larger dataset (file: *SORT*, SORTBY sheet) and captured by Figure 6-12.

name	soc	phil	poli sci	art	physics	chem		eng
Ted	66	66	70	35	76	90		
Said	36	83	30	42	66	56		
Maureen	75	49	89	72	98	79		
Vincenza	41	85	53	75	61	45		
Chen	61	38	46	36	57	66		56
Clothilde	59	52	100	94	38	31		87
Hiran	55	68	87	47	56	50		98
Agnieska	84	97	35	52	75	86		55
Paolo	34	80	81	56	57	64		77
Haseem	71	59	69	61	100	72		61
								84
								68
								90
								80

Figure 6-12. *Field relation, once removed: the eng field is detached from the dataset*

In spite of eng's independence from the dataset, it can nevertheless drive a sort of the student names:

$$=SORTBY(name,eng,-1)$$

as we see in Figure 6-13.

=SORTBY(name,eng,-1)
Maureen
Paolo
Said
Hiran
Chen
Agnieska
Clothilde
Ted
Vincenza
Haseem

Figure 6-13. *The field that is, and isn't, there: student names sorted by the eng field*

You'll note that the eng score of 98 is notched in the third row of the field, corresponding to Maureen's position in the *name* field – the third row. Thus the two fields are made to line up, even as they're distanced by columns and rows. And that teaches us in turn that in order for that line-up and ensuing sort to happen, the two fields must possess the same number of rows.

Note   We'll later see that the powerful HSTACK function can easily reposition the name and eng fields next to one another, building a new dataset.

And note in addition that SORTBY stipulates that sort-by field(s) be identified by their name (or range coordinates, absent a field name), but for SORT, the sort-by fields must appear as a *sort index*. Thus the 2 in the formula

=SORT(All,2)

refers to the second column in the dataset; but because SORTBY grants the user the freedom to sort by a column that's *independent* of any dataset, a sort index can't work there because it wouldn't know to which column a "2" would refer.

Note   Once you call upon a second (or additional) field in SORTBY, that field's "sort order" argument *must* be entered. Thus this syntax would be required, for example, =SORTBY(Salesperson,,Country,-1). Here, the 1 cannot be omitted from the second-field argument.

Coming Next

Sorting data is one of the spreadsheet essentials, and the two dynamic array SORT functions take the business of sorting to another order of magnitude, pun intended. Now we're moving on to review another mission-critical entry in Excel's job description, one that's also been treated to a grand, dynamic makeover – in the form of the FILTER function.

CHAPTER 7

The FILTER Function: Cutting the Data Down to Size

Your dataset may be an embarrassment of riches, but sometimes more is less. Every spreadsheet user knows that their data often warehouses more information than they need right now, and could do with a bit of incisive, if temporary, trimming.

And Excel's new dynamic array FILTER function is very much up to that task. And as with SORT and SORTBY, FILTER contributes a set of formula-centered solutions to a classic spreadsheet chore that's been handled heretofore by a potpourri of tools, for example, pivot table filters and slicers, the Advanced Filter option, and the standard-issue Filter you see atop tables and the like.

They all have their place, of course, but because FILTER does its thing with formulas, a vast catalog of criteria by which the data can be summoned becomes available, making FILTER a most powerful and exceedingly agile means for getting what you want from the data. FILTER is the dynamic array's Swiss army knife – it can slice and dice the data in so many ways.

The Formula

FILTER comprises three arguments, the final one of which is optional (but useful):

$$=FILTER(range/array,include,if\_empty)$$

The first argument, again officially dubbed "array" by Excel, calls for the dataset you want to filter, and of course accepts range or table names in lieu of cell coordinates.

© Abbott Ira Katz 2023
A. I. Katz, *Up Up and Array!*, https://doi.org/10.1007/978-1-4842-8966-2_7

It's the second argument – "include" – from which FILTER's power radiates. Start with an elementary filter (file: *FILTER*, adapted from fellow Apress author Debra Dalgliesh's Contexture compendium of free downloads, Again, the dataset in its entirety is called All).

We want to filter the food-sales dataset for all sales conducted in Boston. Enter Boston in L1 and follow in L3 with

=FILTER(All,City=L1)

You should see as follows (again, in excerpt) per Figure 7-1.

=FILTER(all,City=L1)							
43831	East	Boston	Bars	Carrot	33	1.77	58.41
43834	East	Boston	Crackers	Whole Wheat	87	3.49	303.63
43843	East	Boston	Cookies	Arrowroot	38	2.18	82.84
43846	East	Boston	Bars	Carrot	54	1.77	95.58
43849	East	Boston	Crackers	Whole Wheat	149	3.49	520.01
43861	East	Boston	Cookies	Arrowroot	36	2.18	78.48
43864	East	Boston	Cookies	Chocolate Chip	31	1.87	57.97
43867	East	Boston	Crackers	Whole Wheat	28	3.49	97.72
43879	East	Boston	Cookies	Arrowroot	43	2.18	93.74
43882	East	Boston	Cookies	Oatmeal Raisin	123	2.84	349.32
43898	East	Boston	Bars	Carrot	61	1.77	107.97
43901	East	Boston	Crackers	Whole Wheat	40	3.49	139.6
43916	East	Boston	Bars	Bran	103	1.87	192.61
43919	East	Boston	Cookies	Oatmeal Raisin	193	2.84	548.12
43937	East	Boston	Bars	Carrot	48	1.77	84.96
43940	East	Boston	Snacks	Potato Chips	134	1.68	225.12
43955	East	Boston	Bars	Bran	105	1.87	196.35

Figure 7-1. *Bean counting: food sales in Beantown*

(Again, as with SORT, the resulting spill range evinces basic, default formatting that you'd almost surely want to modify; and again, the results are header-free. That row could be copied and pasted atop the spill range.)

We've successfully isolated all the sales conducted in Boston, and with that achievement in hand let's return to FILTER's syntax. Here the "include" argument

City=L1

cites the name of the field doing the filtering and asks the dataset to search for whatever city name we've written to L1. You've doubtless inferred, then, that if we substitute New York for Boston in L1, all of the former city's sales will be returned by the filter. And you could probably deduce in turn that if we were to enter Cookies in L1, we'd need to rewrite our formula in L4 to read

=FILTER(All,Category=L1)

because Cookies is an item populating that field.

These basic FILTER constructions are pretty straightforward but rather powerful just the same – because you can conduct rapid-fire analyses of the sales in any city or activity for any food category by simply substituting the desired item in L1. And notice that while our formulas have imposed a condition of sorts on the data – for example, filter a record only if its city matches Boston – FILTER criteria *never* require use of the word IF. You only enter the *condition(s) itself* – what IF formulas call a logical test – and nothing more. Thus FILTERs never ask you to post a criterion – that is, an "include" argument – that begins

=IF(Category=L1...

Now About That [If Empty] Argument

Before we explore more of FILTER's most important criteria variations, let's not forget the function's optional If Empty argument. If Empty plays a cosmetic role in the filtering enterprise, letting the user supply an info notification to the formula, in the event the filter turns up nothing. Thus, if I enter Tacos in L1 – an item nowhere to be found in the Category field – FILTER will default to an unsightly #CALC! exclamation. But if I edit FILTER to read

=FILTER(All,Category=L1,"Not found")

That caption will replace the error message.

Multiple Filter Criteria: Getting More (or Less) Out of the Data

Now suppose we want to filter the data for Cookies sales in San Diego. That's an objective, of course, that requires two criteria – one each drawn from the Category and City fields. With that two-pronged intention in mind we can now enter San Diego in M1, and go on to edit our filter formula to read

$$=FILTER(All,(Category=L1)*(City=M1),"Not found")$$

The formula has assumed two new elements, both of which are integral to a multi-criteria filter. First, once a second (or third, etc.) criterion enters the formula, each criterion must be surrounded by its own pair of parentheses. Second, recognize that we've in effect written an AND statement. That is, we're insisting that the formula nail down all the records in which the Category field reports the entry Cookie *and* the City field lists San Diego. The means for stipulating "and" in a filter formula is the asterisk, wedged in between the criteria. And so if you needed to import a third criteria, the syntax would look like this:

$$(1^{st} criterion)*(2^{nd} criterion)*(3^{rd} criterion)$$

(In fact, the asterisk – Excel's multiplier operator – is actually performing an act of multiplication inside the formula, too, but we can skim past the details of that maneuver here.)

Once we've gotten all that punctuation in place, we should see the following, per Figure 7-2.

=FILTER(all,(Category=L1)*(City=M1),"Not found")

43895	West	San Diego	Cookies	Oatmeal Raisin	30	2.84	85.2
43913	West	San Diego	Cookies	Chocolate Chip	39	1.87	72.93
43952	West	San Diego	Cookies	Chocolate Chip	63	1.87	117.81
43973	West	San Diego	Cookies	Chocolate Chip	55	1.87	102.85
44057	West	San Diego	Cookies	Chocolate Chip	70	1.87	130.9
44147	West	San Diego	Cookies	Arrowroot	103	2.18	224.54
44150	West	San Diego	Cookies	Oatmeal Raisin	32	2.84	90.88
44168	West	San Diego	Cookies	Arrowroot	139	2.18	303.02
44171	West	San Diego	Cookies	Oatmeal Raisin	29	2.84	82.36
44195	West	San Diego	Cookies	Arrowroot	83	2.18	180.94
44243	West	San Diego	Cookies	Oatmeal Raisin	29	2.84	82.36
44308	West	San Diego	Cookies	Chocolate Chip	67	1.87	125.29
44329	West	San Diego	Cookies	Chocolate Chip	82	1.87	153.34
44344	West	San Diego	Cookies	Arrowroot	36	2.18	78.48
44347	West	San Diego	Cookies	Oatmeal Raisin	44	2.84	124.96
44413	West	San Diego	Cookies	Arrowroot	90	2.18	196.2
44416	West	San Diego	Cookies	Oatmeal Raisin	38	2.84	107.92

Figure 7-2. *San Diego snacking: a two-criteria filter*

OR Consider This Alternative

Now let's assume instead that you want to filter all the food sales for *both* San Diego and Los Angeles, your west coast accounts. That is, we're seeking records for sales conducted in *either* San Diego *or* Los Angeles. If we enter Los Angeles in L1 to accompany the San Diego in M1, and amend our formula to

=FILTER(All,(City=L1)+(City=M1),"Not found")

You should see the following, as in Figure 7-3.

=FILTER(All,(City=L1)+(City=M1),"Not found")

43837	West	Los Angeles	Cookies	Chocolate Chip	58	1.87	108.46
43852	West	Los Angeles	Bars	Carrot	51	1.77	90.27
43870	West	Los Angeles	Bars	Carrot	44	1.77	77.88
43885	West	Los Angeles	Bars	Bran	42	1.87	78.54
43888	West	Los Angeles	Cookies	Oatmeal Raisin	33	2.84	93.72
43895	West	San Diego	Cookies	Oatmeal Raisin	30	2.84	85.2
43904	West	Los Angeles	Cookies	Chocolate Chip	86	1.87	160.82
43913	West	San Diego	Cookies	Chocolate Chip	39	1.87	72.93
43922	West	Los Angeles	Bars	Carrot	58	1.77	102.66
43925	West	Los Angeles	Snacks	Potato Chips	68	1.68	114.24
43934	West	San Diego	Snacks	Potato Chips	28	1.68	47.04
43943	West	Los Angeles	Bars	Carrot	20	1.77	35.4
43952	West	San Diego	Cookies	Chocolate Chip	63	1.87	117.81
43961	West	Los Angeles	Bars	Carrot	25	1.77	44.25
43964	West	Los Angeles	Crackers	Whole Wheat	21	3.49	73.29
43973	West	San Diego	Cookies	Chocolate Chip	55	1.87	102.85
43985	West	Los Angeles	Cookies	Oatmeal Raisin	288	2.84	817.92

Figure 7-3. *California comestibles: food sales in Los Angeles and San Diego*

What clearly distinguishes the multi-criteria "or" filter from an "and" is a swap of the asterisk for the plus sign – nothing more.

Mix and Match: AND and OR Together

Next question: what if you want to filter for all the Cookies sales in both Los Angeles and San Diego? That's a tasty problem, to be sure, requisitioning as it does both "and" as well as "or" criteria. Here, I want the filter to detect sales compiled in either Los Angeles or San Diego – but only of Cookies. How is this one written?

Like this:

=FILTER(All,((City=L1)+(City=M1))*(Category=N1),"Not found")

An extra brace of parentheses now hugs both halves of the "or" expression, treating it all as a unitary result that proceeds to work with the "and" statement. If you inadvertently forget the second parentheses around the two City references, the formula will first consider criteria 1 and 2 alone, and *then* criteria 2 and 3 alone, thus mining outcomes that won't necessarily fulfill *all* the criteria at the same time (but if you've been clicking along, you'll note that all the San Diego entries *will* be coupled with Cookies, for example,

$$(City=M1))*(Category=N1)$$

because those pairings always call upon criteria 2 and 3, as they're *adjacent*. But the Los Angeles records aren't invariably matched with Cookies, because that city occupies criterion 1, and isn't directly associated with criterion 3, the Category reference.)

In any case, once you put every bit and piece in its place Figure 7-4 lets you know what you should be seeing the following.

=FILTER(All,((City=L1)+(City=M1))*(Category=N1),"Not found")							
43837	West	Los Angeles	Cookies	Chocolate Chip	58	1.87	108.46
43888	West	Los Angeles	Cookies	Oatmeal Raisin	33	2.84	93.72
43895	West	San Diego	Cookies	Oatmeal Raisin	30	2.84	85.2
43904	West	Los Angeles	Cookies	Chocolate Chip	86	1.87	160.82
43913	West	San Diego	Cookies	Chocolate Chip	39	1.87	72.93
43952	West	San Diego	Cookies	Chocolate Chip	63	1.87	117.81
43973	West	San Diego	Cookies	Chocolate Chip	55	1.87	102.85
43985	West	Los Angeles	Cookies	Oatmeal Raisin	288	2.84	817.92
44027	West	Los Angeles	Cookies	Chocolate Chip	75	1.87	140.25
44048	West	Los Angeles	Cookies	Chocolate Chip	107	1.87	200.09
44057	West	San Diego	Cookies	Chocolate Chip	70	1.87	130.9
44069	West	Los Angeles	Cookies	Chocolate Chip	80	1.87	149.6
44147	West	San Diego	Cookies	Arrowroot	103	2.18	224.54
44150	West	San Diego	Cookies	Oatmeal Raisin	32	2.84	90.88
44168	West	San Diego	Cookies	Arrowroot	139	2.18	303.02
44171	West	San Diego	Cookies	Oatmeal Raisin	29	2.84	82.36
44195	West	San Diego	Cookies	Arrowroot	83	2.18	180.94

Figure 7-4. *Cal. Counting: Cookies sales in Los Angeles and San Diego*

Now let's return to our inaugural FILTER formula, the one in which we returned the sales data for Boston. By definition, then, all our results there must disclose that city's name in the City field – and precisely because that field will contain nothing but Boston, we don't really need all that redundant information. As a result, and for good presentational reasons, we might want to eject the City field from this filter – and in order to make good on that intention we can reprise the INDEX formula we dusted off in Chapter 5, in the course of our perusal of the UNIQUE function.

Here, our formula reads

=FILTER(INDEX(All,SEQUENCE(ROWS(All)),{1,2,4,5,6,7,8}),City=M1,"Not found")

Don't be fooled or confused; in spite of its density, the filter here consists of the same three arguments with which we've been working all along. The INDEX formula is assembling an improvised dataset, one appropriating the All minus the City field – the third column in All, thus explaining the missing 3 in the bracketed array. Note in addition the SEQUENCE function here that's performing the same work it did in the UNIQUE formula – it's counting, and hence including, all of the rows in the All dataset.

And once you're satisfied with your formula, the results should follow corroborated by Figure 7-5.

=FILTER(INDEX(All,SEQUENCE(ROWS(All)),{1,2,4,5,6,7,8}),City=M1,"Not found")						
43831	East	Bars	Carrot	33	1.8	58.41
43834	East	Crackers	Whole Wheat	87	3.5	303.63
43843	East	Cookies	Arrowroot	38	2.2	82.84
43846	East	Bars	Carrot	54	1.8	95.58
43849	East	Crackers	Whole Wheat	149	3.5	520.01
43861	East	Cookies	Arrowroot	36	2.2	78.48
43864	East	Cookies	Chocolate Chip	31	1.9	57.97
43867	East	Crackers	Whole Wheat	28	3.5	97.72
43879	East	Cookies	Arrowroot	43	2.2	93.74
43882	East	Cookies	Oatmeal Raisin	123	2.8	349.32
43898	East	Bars	Carrot	61	1.8	107.97
43901	East	Crackers	Whole Wheat	40	3.5	139.6
43916	East	Bars	Bran	103	1.9	192.61
43919	East	Cookies	Oatmeal Raisin	193	2.8	548.12
43937	East	Bars	Carrot	48	1.8	84.96
43940	East	Snacks	Potato Chips	134	1.7	225.12
43955	East	Bars	Bran	105	1.9	196.35

Figure 7-5. *Something's missing – on purpose. The City field isn't there.*

All those Bostons are gone; and for good measure, we could have zapped the Region field, too – the dataset's second field – from the formula, by excising the 2 from the bracketed array – because, after all, Boston is always in the East.

Note   Our discussion of the new dynamic array function DROP in a later chapter will describe a considerably more elegant way in which this result can be achieved

---

How About Filtering Part of a Cell?

Thus far, we've learned about filtering fields whose data consists of single words, for example, Cookies, or Boston. But what about cells consisting of what's typically called unstructured text – that is, multi-word content taking up residence in a single cell address? Can FILTER help us to unearth a keyword, or selected words from the larger text sitting in a cell?

Well, the answer is a decisive yes. FILTER can masterfully extract partial text excerpts from a range of cells, and for a case in point break open the *FILTER – text search* file, an adaptation of a spreadsheet that enumerates the current members of the House of Representatives (source: Everypolitican (`https://everypolitician.org/united-states-of-america/house/download.html`)).

Suppose for starters we want to filter the name field for all Representatives named John. The problem, of course, is that all the names are bunched into single cells – first, last, and middle names – and we need to somehow uproot "John" from the lengthier entries into which the name has been gathered.

To give that assignment a go we'll tap into the SEARCH function, an old but robust means for discovering the morsels of text cooking in a larger stew of words. SEARCH is what I call a positional function, because it delivers a *number* corresponding to the position in a cell at which the searched text begins, assuming it's found. Thus if I search for the word Thursday in the cell entry "Today is Thursday" SEARCH will offer up 10, the position number of the T in Thursday. It's written as follows:

=SEARCH(find_text,within_text,start_number)

The start number argument is optional.

Thus if "Today is Thursday" is written to A6 and we enter Thursday in A2, this formula

=SEARCH(A2,A6)

will pump out 10. If the searched text isn't there, a #VALUE! error message will stake the cell instead. Remember, of course, that we're about to apply SEARCH to an entire *range* of names, but we're in dynamic array mode, and that's something we can do.

Now back to our task. In the FILTER tab of the *FILTER – text search* workbook enter John in B2. In B4, write

=FILTER(name,ISNUMBER(SEARCH(B2,name)),"Not found")

The ISNUMBER function wrapping itself around SEARCH tests a value or formula for its numeric status; thus if a search of each cell in the name range yields a number – meaning that the search term has been found – that cell will instate itself into the filtered result.

Our FILTER thus looks like this, per Figure 7-6.

John			
=FILTER(name,ISNUMBER(SEARCH(B2,name)),"Not found")			
Bill Johnson			
Dusty Johnson			
Eddie Bernice Johnson			
Henry C. "Hank" Johnson, Jr.			
John A. Yarmuth			
John B. Larson			
John Garamendi			
John H. Rutherford			
John Joyce			
John Katko			
John Lewis			
John P. Sarbanes			
John R. Carter			
John R. Curtis			
John R. Moolenaar			
John Ratcliffe			
John Shimkus			
John W. Rose			
Mike Johnson			

Figure 7-6. *Restricted entry: Congresspersons with John in their name – somewhere in their name*

That works – sort of. But we see that our filter has garnered a trio of Johnsons – which also contain the text John – that we probably didn't have in mind. A workaround: enter in B2 instead

John[space]

That search term will close the door on the Johnsons, simply because the John in their names is succeeded by a character other than [space]. That second take will yield as follows, illustrated in Figure 7-7.

John		
=FILTER(name,ISNUMBER(SEARCH(B2,name)),"Not found"		
John A. Yarmuth		
John B. Larson		
John Garamendi		
John H. Rutherford		
John Joyce		
John Katko		
John Lewis		
John P. Sarbanes		
John R. Carter		
John R. Curtis		
John R. Moolenaar		
John Ratcliffe		
John Shimkus		
John W. Rose		

Figure 7-7. *That's more like it: nothing but John*

Thus we see that FILTER does a superior job of performing text/keyword searches of free, or unstructured, text – a most flexible and dynamic capability.

Note   Some approaches to dividing last and first names into distinct cells will be explored when we review Excel's newest dynamic array functions TEXTBEFORE and TEXTAFTER.

There's More

In fact, FILTER's potential is in large measure curtailed only by the smarts you bring to your formulas. Another example, just for demo's sake: suppose we wanted to be able to return all the names of Congresspersons starting with a particular letter. Say now I enter B in B2 and rewrite B4's formula to read

=FILTER(name,LEFT(name,1)=B2)

Here the LEFT function peels the first letter from each name, and FILTER takes over and winnows the ones starting with the initial you've entered in B2, recorded in Figure 7-8.

B
=FILTER(name,LEFT(name,1)=B2)
Barbara Lee
Barry Loudermilk
Ben Cline
Ben McAdams
Ben Ray LujÃin
Bennie G. Thompson
Betty McCollum
Bill Flores
Bill Foster
Bill Huizenga
Bill Johnson
Bill Pascrell, Jr.
Bill Posey
Billy Long
Blaine Luetkemeyer
Bob Gibbs
Bobby L. Rush
Bonnie Watson Coleman

Figure 7-8. *Initial success*

And remember, in addition to many other possibilities, I could write in another cell

=COUNTA(B4#)

to deliver a total of members of Congress with names beginning with the designated letter.

FILTER's Number Wizardry Adds Values to Your Values

And of course, FILTER is at your service should you need to count the numbers. By way of a simple example, let's call up a familiar-looking dataset, here stored in the *FILTER: Values* file.

We want, at least by way of a first look, to filter all order amounts there equalling or exceeding $2,000. Let's enter 2000 in cell H3 and follow in H5 with

=FILTER(All,Order_Amount>=H3)

That expression should be pretty clear. We're attempting to filter the entire dataset All by order amounts that equal or surpass the value we've entered in H3. Working with 2000 you should see the following, per Figure 7-9.

2000				
=FILTER(all,Order_Amount>=H3)				
France	Buchanan	43612	10249	2365.76
Mexico	Peacock	43612	10250	3597.9
Mexico	Peacock	43639	10266	3536.6
Canada	Leverling	43645	10271	2037.28
Canada	Callahan	43663	10285	3016
Canada	Callahan	43667	10288	2169
Mexico	Fuller	43672	10297	3055
Canada	Callahan	43673	10298	3740
France	Suyama	43675	10308	2645
Canada	Davolio	43698	10323	2094.3
UK	Davolio	43702	10325	2835
Mexico	Callahan	43703	10326	3741.3

Figure 7-9. Making the number: sales equalling or bettering $2000

(Remember that the greater and less-than operators always precede the = sign in Excel formulas.)

Now for another value-driven task, what if you need to study all the sales conducted, say, between January 1, 2020, and June 30 of that year – that is, a 6-month summary?

Ok. This time enter 1/1/2020 in H3 and follow in I3 with 6/30/2020. Write, in H5

=FILTER(all,(Order_Date>=H3)*(Order_Date<=I3))

Again, this is an AND formula, because the filtered dates must satisfy both criteria. And as such, each criterion need be flanked by parentheses and separated by the asterisk befitting "and" filters. Write that formula and you should see the following (I've formatted the Order_Date in order to clarify the results here) (viewed in excerpt, in Figure 7-10).

=FILTER(all,(Order_Date>=H3)*(Order_Date<=I3))				
UK	Callahan	1/1/2020	10447	517.44
Canada	Leverling	1/1/2020	10448	454
Mexico	Suyama	1/1/2020	10449	360
UK	Leverling	1/5/2020	10450	1792
UK	Suyama	1/6/2020	10451	246.24
UK	Leverling	1/7/2020	10452	174.9
France	Leverling	1/8/2020	10453	1031.7
Canada	Peacock	1/11/2020	10454	443.4
Canada	Suyama	1/11/2020	10455	1020
UK	Peacock	1/12/2020	10456	331.2
France	Callahan	1/13/2020	10457	2018.5
Mexico	Davolio	1/13/2020	10458	407.7
UK	Leverling	1/14/2020	10459	1838.2
UK	Callahan	1/15/2020	10460	557.6
France	Peacock	1/15/2020	10461	4924.13
Mexico	Peacock	1/15/2020	10462	1659.2
Canada	Callahan	1/19/2020	10463	2684
Canada	Callahan	1/19/2020	10464	176.1

Figure 7-10. *Half a year's worth of sales*

Note   You can also enter date criteria via this slightly more ponderous method, for example, =FILTER(All,Order_Date=VALUE("6/10/2013"))

No More Blank Looks About Blank Rows

If you're looking for a data-quality conundrum that can make the day of any spreadsheet analyst big time, start with blank rows. These nullities are the bane of conventional sorting, pivot tables, and traditional filters, but once you get with the FILTER program you can actually do real work – even if you leave those blanks in place.

By way of example, here's a modification of a spreadsheet (File: *Filter – working with blank rows*) released by a New York City agency (for the original file go here

https://media.githubusercontent.com/media/thecityny/housing-lottery-data/
master/housing-lotteries.csv)), one that itemizes public housing apartments offered
up via a lottery. Its blank rows as you see them, however, came that way in the original
sheet. So what can we do? (As usual, the dataset is entitled All, and the field names
derive from the header row.)

Here's what. Suppose we want to filter the Rent field for all properties priced at $800
a month or less. Turn to the Filter worksheet (note that in the interests of clarity I've
proactively pasted the headers in row 6, to point to the Rent field). Enter, in B7 and as
embodied by Figure 7-11.

$$=FILTER(All,Rent<=B3)$$

800															
=FILTER(All,Rent<=B3)															
Lottery Number	Project Na	PHN	Street Nai	Boro	NC/Pres	Oversight	Unit Size	Rent		Number o	Eligible H	income_n	income_n	hh_size2	income_n	income_n h
0	0	0	0	0	0	0	0	0	0	0	0	0	0	0	0
82	Rufus Kin	148-15	90 AVE	4	New Cons	HPD	0	659	1	1	24515	30100			
0	0	0	0	0	0	0	0	0	0	0	0	0	0	0	0
0	0	0	0	0	0	0	0	0	0	0	0	0	0	0	0
82	Rufus Kin	148-15	90 AVE	4	New Cons	HPD	1	709	2	1	26298	30100	2	26298	34400
0	0	0	0	0	0	0	0	0	0	0	0	0	0	0	0
0	0	0	0	0	0	0	0	0	0	0	0	0	0	0	0
0	0	0	0	0	0	0	0	0	0	0	0	0	0	0	0
83	Norman T	90-14	161 STREE	4	New Cons	HDC	0	500	1	1	19406	29400			
0	0	0	0	0	0	0	0	0	0	0	0	0	0	0	0
0	0	0	0	0	0	0	0	0	0	0	0	0	0	0	0
0	0	0	0	0	0	0	0	0	0	0	0	0	0	0	0
83	Norman T	90-14	161 STREE	4	New Cons	HDC	1	516	3	1	20023	23520	2	20023	26880
0	0	0	0	0	0	0	0	0	0	0	0	0	0	0	0
83	Norman T	90-14	161 STREE	4	New Cons	HDC	1	640	11	1	24275	29400	2	24275	33600
0	0	0	0	0	0	0	0	0	0	0	0	0	0	0	0

Figure 7-11. *Probably not what you had in mind: Rent-free properties?*

And we get the following, in excerpt, in Figure 7-11.

Now that doesn't look right, does it? But the problem is that the filter was constructed
correctly; it has properly turned up all the rents that meet our criterion – equal to or
less than $800. But remember that every other row in our data set is blank, and as such
their Rent field naturally evaluates to 0 – and 0 is less than 800. What we want, then, is a
formulaic take two, something like this:

$$=FILTER(All,(Rent<=B3)*(Rent<>0))$$

yielding as follows, in Figure 7-12.

| =FILTER(All,(Rent<=B3)*(Rent<>0)) | | | | | | | | | | | | | | |
Lottery Number	Project Na	PHN	Street Nai	Boro	NC/Pres	Oversight	Unit Size	Rent	Number o	Eligible H	income_n	income_n	hh_size2	income_n	income_n
82	Rufus Kin	148-15	90 AVE	4	New Cons	HPD	0	659	1	1	24515	30100			
82	Rufus Kin	148-15	90 AVE	4	New Cons	HPD	1	709	2	1	26298	30100	2	26298	34400
83	Norman T	90-14	161 STREE	4	New Cons	HDC	0	500	1	1	19406	29400			
83	Norman T	90-14	161 STREE	4	New Cons	HDC	1	516	3	1	20023	23520	2	20023	26880
83	Norman T	90-14	161 STREE	4	New Cons	HDC	1	640	11	1	24275	29400	2	24275	33600
83	Norman T	90-14	161 STREE	4	New Cons	HDC	2	774	5	2	28938	33600	3	28938	37800
85	Morris Co	253	EAST 142 S	2	New Cons	HDC	0	785	24	1	28595	35280			
88	Utica Plac	1339	LINCOLN F	3	New Cons	HDC	0	494	18	1	18618	23520			
88	Utica Plac	1339	LINCOLN F	3	New Cons	HDC	0	785	5	1	28595	35280			
89	Harlem W	24	WEST 117	1	New Cons	HPD	0	491	9	1	19637	23520			
89	Harlem W	24	WEST 117	1	New Cons	HPD	0	635	3	1	24873	29400			
89	Harlem W	24	WEST 117	1	New Cons	HPD	1	528	7	1	21019	23520	2	21019	26880
89	Harlem W	24	WEST 117	1	New Cons	HPD	1	682	3	1	26619	29400	2	26619	33600
89	Harlem W	24	WEST 117	1	New Cons	HPD	2	643	2	2	25273	26880	3	25273	30240
90	Knickerbo	803	KNICKERB	3	New Cons	HPD	1	689	1	1	25338	29400	2	25338	33600
91	Crossroad	535	UNION AV	2	New Cons	HDC	0	494	1	1	18618	23520			
91	Crossroad	535	UNION AV	2	New Cons	HDC	0	785	1	1	28595	35280			

Figure 7-12. *That's more like it*

Coming Next

Sure, filtering a dataset half of whose rows contain absolutely nothing in them sounds a touch gimmicky, but you get the idea – and besides, we've been working here with an actual spreadsheet. The FILTER function can crunch a subset of your data that meets just about any specification, and the more specifications you can imagine, the more powerful the function. Next up is a very different dynamic array function that performs a very different set of tasks – RANDARRAY.

CHAPTER 8

RANDARRAY: Unpredictably Useful

Has anyone noticed that RANDARRY is the only dynamic array function that's actually smuggled the word "array" into its name? My explanation for that curiosity isn't likely to stir you with its profundity. My take is that Excel had to differentiate RANDARRY from its random-number-generating predecessors RAND and RANDBETWEEN, and ARRAY seems like a perfectly good and descriptive term to pair with RAND this time.

Yes, RANDARRY does generate dynamic arrays, and swiftly and easily, though its user-friendliness doesn't address the obvious prior question: when would I use it?

How It's Written

First, let's see how RANDARRAY works. It comprises five arguments, all of which are actually optional – though of course you have to use at least one of them:

=RANDARRY(rows,column,min,max,integer)

If, for starters, I write

=RANDARRAY(10)

I'll order up a ten-row array spilling values that look like this, as conveyed in Figure 8-1.

A. I. Katz, *Up Up and Array!*, https://doi.org/10.1007/978-1-4842-8966-2_8

=RANDARRAY(10)
0.611384
0.819586
0.537253
0.247374
0.558203
0.990322
0.886085
0.877243
0.361291
0.422315

Figure 8-1. *Somewhere between 0 and 1: a ten-row random array*

We see then that, as a matter of default, the randomized values span the narrow gamut between 0 and 1. Write

=RANDARRAY(,10)

with that comma in evidence, and the values spill across ten columns, much in the way the SEQUENCE negotiates row and column-generated spills. Write this expression, however:

=RANDARRAY(10,10)

And you'll have drawn a rectangle of values, 10-by-10, presented in Figure 8-2.

=RANDARRAY(10,10)									
0.130319	0.577796	0.226195	0.23342	0.584818	0.254906	0.3301	0.413218	0.213716	0.859
0.061831	0.329003	0.800465	0.252711	0.039681	0.15037	0.718492	0.149739	0.222166	0.339906
0.493927	0.869111	0.850901	0.00326	0.919745	0.723301	0.392539	0.613767	0.523449	0.875203
0.964514	0.849643	0.377129	0.311725	0.654884	0.37109	0.174845	0.840718	0.178042	0.952174
0.100019	0.959383	0.938221	0.905891	0.268314	0.064536	0.86928	0.942461	0.139307	0.33201
0.672169	0.086015	0.461811	0.5901	0.813756	0.45866	0.342214	0.914257	0.642695	0.544121
0.618017	0.516531	0.744248	0.653838	0.635137	0.59761	0.418884	0.958003	0.042563	0.266728
0.634747	0.77588	0.088491	0.982235	0.256731	0.790873	0.752576	0.20721	0.289922	0.516372
0.919789	0.526138	0.026835	0.864672	0.939323	0.727292	0.976368	0.083851	0.022998	0.212425
0.928469	0.367403	0.03778	0.448241	0.79263	0.124355	0.333663	0.416576	0.003995	0.45881

Figure 8-2. *A century of random values*

Now because the spill range is formula-propelled, all its values will change with every refresh of the spreadsheet (and that includes any additional data entry, at least by default). If you need to freeze those values – and you very well might – you can select the entire RANDARRY spill range and perform a Copy > Paste Values.

And if you don't like all those decimals, you can avail yourself of RANDARRAY's third, fourth, and fifth arguments. If I write

=RANDARRAY(10,10,1,10,1)

the formula will spread out ten columns and rows and generate values ranging between 1 and 10, with that final 1 signifying an integer (whole number) argument (you could also write TRUE in lieu of 1, but you probably won't). Figure 8-3 demonstrates what I mean.

=RANDARRAY(10,10,1,10,1)									
9	2	3	4	5	5	1	3	5	1
9	2	5	10	9	2	7	6	9	7
6	6	10	2	5	4	10	3	6	5
1	9	8	6	10	6	5	7	10	10
1	7	10	5	6	7	10	1	2	2
2	4	2	3	3	1	8	2	8	5
6	5	1	6	1	8	8	4	2	3
3	8	9	4	3	2	10	8	6	5
2	5	3	8	4	7	1	8	3	3
3	9	2	8	2	8	4	2	3	8

Figure 8-3. *A whole lot of whole numbers*

Note   Statistical pundits maintain that Excel's randomizing functions aren't truly random, but yet for nearly all practical purposes they're equal to the randomizing task. For a technical consideration of some of the issues look <u>here</u>.)

Some Uses, Please

Still, our prior question needs to be asked again: when would you use RANDARRAY?

Here's one potential application. Suppose you're a teacher who needs to design a four-option, 50-question multiple choice exam, and you want to protect yourself from falling into some inadvertent pattern, one that would arouse the interest of a student who's looking for any clue to the answers. With that intention in mind, you could enter

$$=RANDARRAY(50,,1,4,1)$$

That formula will unroll 50 rows' worth of random values falling between 1 and 4. If the results make you nervous – if, for example, one stretch of the answers contains too many consecutive 2's – just refresh the spreadsheet and inspect it again. Once you're happy with the distribution, freeze the answers with a Copy > Paste Values.

But what if your exam offers not four numbered alternatives per question, but rather an *alphabetical* answer scheme – A through D?

You could do the following: Say you've entered your 50-question answers RANDARRAY formula in A5, the formula currently spilling values 1 through 4. Next construct a small lookup range (which again, Microsoft insists on calling it a table array), say beginning in G5, in which the values are poised to lookup their alpha equivalent, per Figure 8-4.

1	A
2	B
3	C
4	D

Figure 8-4. *Alpha-numeric exchange*

Name the range score, and enter in B5

$$=VLOOKUP(A5\#,score,2)$$

Again, remember that A5# refers to the original RANDARRAY formula. The lookup examines every value in the A column and replaces it with the alpha entry populating the second column of the lookup range. You should see something like Figure 8-5.

=VLOOKUP(A5#,score,2)
2 B
1 A
4 D
4 D
2 B
2 B
1 A
2 B
4 D
4 D
2 B
4 D
1 A
1 A
2 B
2 B
4 D
2 B
2 B
3 C

Figure 8-5. *Letter perfect*

"Something like" the above screen shot, because if you've been clicking along, your randomized set of values won't resemble the one above. And if you're happy with that answer distribution, you can proceed to a Copy > Paste Values and finalize the answers.

Another pedagogical possibility: you're scheduling a test and want to randomize the seating of your students (practice file: *RANDARRAY – student names*). You can enter, in the column adjoining your list of student names (here range-named class), this formula:

=SORTBY(class,RANDARRAY(COUNTA(class)))

That expression calls for a bit of review, as it returns us to the SORTBY function. We're sorting the student names inhabiting the range class by a randomized set of values which *won't appear in the spreadsheet.* Remember that SORTBY can sort a range/array by another range that's entirely *independent* of the data to be sorted – it needn't be adjacent to the sorted data, nor even committed to spreadsheet cells at all. Here the sort-by field comprises ten randomized values confined to the brain of the formula, and that's fine; SORTBY will work, nevertheless. (We're also not bothered by the RANDARRAY outputs of those default decimal values – we just need ten random numbers, which we're not actually viewing in any case.)

Get the formula right and you should see something like Figure 8-6.

	=SORTBY(class,RANDARRAY(COUNTA(class)))		
Billy	Zelda		
Jane	Emily		
Ted	Billy		
Emily	Arlene		
Roger	Sal		
Cathy	Jane		
Sal	Roger		
Arlene	Vance		
Zelda	Cathy		
Vance	Ted		

Figure 8-6. *No-cheating seating: randomizing student positions in the classroom*

Again, of course, your seating sequence will almost surely depart from the above shot, because we're working with RANDARRAY. And again, if you find your results pause-giving – that is, best friends Zelda and Emily have wound up sitting next to one another – just refresh the worksheet until your results achieve a seating distribution that satisfies your needs (we'll see more about seating arrangements in the chapter on WRAPCOLS).

This kind of application of RANDARRAY could also be brought to lotteries, in which ticket numbers could be sorted per the above exercise.

Rolls of the Dice, Virtually

For a final exercise, we can step through a means for generating 1000 hypothetical dice outcomes and tallying the distribution of their outcomes (i.e., the number of 2's, 3's, etc.) – in short, a kind of frequency analysis.

To start, open a blank worksheet and enter in B4

=RANDARRAY(1000,2,1,6,1)

This highly efficient formula fills two 1000-row columns with randomized values ranging from 1 to 6, representing the potential outcomes of the toss of a single die:

=RANDARRAY(1000,2,1,6,1)	
3	2
6	2
6	6
1	1
6	1
6	6
6	4
5	6
5	6
4	3
4	2
2	1
1	3
6	1
4	5
5	2
1	5
1	1
2	6

Figure 8-7. *Las Vegas simulation – dice outcomes, dynamic array style*

Now the next step requires some deeper explanation. We need to calculate the individual, line-by-line outcomes before we calculate the frequencies of the outcomes. Keeping in mind that the outcomes have emerged from one formula in B4, we certainly can't write

=SUM(B4#)

because that expression will simply lasso all 2000 values into one grand total. We need to sum *each row individually*, preparatory to calculating the outcome frequencies. There are several options available to us here, but the shortest looks like this, in D4:

(Again, alternatives are available, but they're lengthier. One such possibility is the BYROW function, a function peculiar to Excel's new LAMBDA formula-development protocol that would take us beyond the purview of this book. But even the BYROW solution is more keystroke-intensive than ours.)

What our formula does is line up the two columns of dice results and perform 1000 iterations of pairwise lifting (remember that?), yielding the individual outcome totals.

=RANDARRAY(1000,2,1,6,1)			
4	3	7	=B4:B1003+C4:C1003
1	4	5	
4	1	5	
6	6	12	
6	4	10	
2	5	7	
4	3	7	
6	5	11	
2	6	8	
4	2	6	
4	2	6	
5	4	9	
5	6	11	
1	2	3	
4	3	7	
1	6	7	
5	6	11	
5	2	7	

Figure 8-8. *Slicing and dicing the outcomes*

Now again, if that looks good, Copy > Paste Values all the results. We'll range-name D4:D1003 dice.

With our results in place, we can go about tabulating the frequencies of outcomes. In H9 enter

=SORT(UNIQUE(dice))

That formula scouts the sums in the D column for unique instances of every outcome and then sorts them in numerical order, per Figure 8-9.

=SORT(UNIQUE(dice))
2
3
4
5
6
7
8
9
10
11
12

Figure 8-9. *Two cubes, eleven outcomes*

(We could have also written =SEQUENCE(11,,2,1) in H9, thus insuring that all 11 dice outcomes would be made available for counting. In theory our UNIQUE formula might omit an outcome or two, if by some extremely remote chance no 2's or 12's were "rolled" by the formula in B4#, for example.)

Now things move in a more conventional direction. We can write in I9

=COUNTIF(dice,H9#)/1000

Format the data in percent terms, and you'll see the following as represented by Figure 8-10.

=SORT(UNIQUE(dice))		
2	2.70%	=COUNTIF(dice,H9#)/1000
3	5.70%	
4	6.50%	
5	12.10%	
6	11.80%	
7	17.20%	
8	13.60%	
9	11.40%	
10	9.20%	
11	7.00%	
12	2.80%	

Figure 8-10. *Playing the percentages: dice outcomes*

Note that if you *don't* fix all the outcomes in the B and C columns via the Copy > Paste Values routine, the results would remain "live," changing with each refresh of the worksheet and thus continually replacing the percentages in the above screen shot with new ones.

Coming Next

We'll have more to say about RANDARRAY, and some ways it can be teamed with Excel's next-generation dynamic functions. But first, let's say a few words – just a few – about a curious function you may never actually use – the implicit intersection operator.

CHAPTER 9

The Implicit Intersection Operator: The Function You'll Probably Never Use

We just said it before, and we'll say it again: you probably won't ever use the intersection operator, for reasons we're about to detail. But the operator is available, just the same; and what the operator – signified by the @ sign – does, for what it's worth, is reduce a dynamic array spilled range to a single-celled output, thus emulating the behavior of formulas in pre-Excel 365 versions.

An example: you'll recall our Beatles range a couple of hundred pages ago cataloging the names of the erstwhile Fab Four. In Excel 365, entering =Beatles will of course spill the names down the column in which the range name was entered. But in Chapter 2 we pointed out that imitating that action in a pre-365 iteration would, by default, only return the *first* entry in the range, issuing under the sway of what's called implicit intersection. As described in that chapter, the only, limited, means for returning all four names would have required the user to select four destination cells at the outset that parallel the projected output of four names, click in the Formula Bar, write =Beatles there, and put the finishing touch on the process by tapping out the storied Ctrl-Shift-Enter sequence, kind of a spreadsheet chord. But since you'd need to select the four cells *before* you proceed, that technique isn't quite of the dynamic array variety.

By way of an additional pre-365 example, if you wanted to multiply three values in A1:A3 by a set of corresponding values in B1:B3, writing =A1:A3*B1:B3 in C1 and pressing Enter, you'd get the following, as in Figure 9-1.

© Abbott Ira Katz 2023
A. I. Katz, *Up Up and Array!*, https://doi.org/10.1007/978-1-4842-8966-2_9

1	4	4 =A1:A3*B1:B3
2	5	
3	6	

Figure 9-1. *Output shortfall: a pre-dynamic array multi-cell multiplication*

1	4	
2	5	10 =A1:A3*B1:B3
3	6	

Figure 9-2. *Same formula, different result*

Now if you deem that result something of a curiosity, writing the same formula in C2, one cell down, would yield

Moreover, even if you were to finalize these formulas with none other than the iconic Ctrl-Shift-Enter, they'd *still* evaluate to a single-celled result.

And for good measure if you were to write the selfsame formula in say, D12, you'd unleash a #VALUE! error message upon the cell.

All these quirky outcomes hinted at the workings of implicit intersection, which, you'll be happy to know, has been consigned to the past tense. Because pre-365 formulas weren't directly capable of outputting multiple results to cells, even when they attempted to, they were forced to decide which *single* result they *would* be able to return. And in formulas such as the ones you see above that result was lined up – literally – with the row on which the formula sat, explaining in turn why a formula entered in D12 would provoke an error message – because row 12 in the worksheet doesn't line up with any of the rows 1 through 3, where the data were positioned. That's implicit intersection – in which the formula is forced to intersect only with the value sharing its row (or column, if the formula were written on the same *column* as the value).

But again, of course, virtually none of this matters now. Dynamic array formulas routinely release their spill range of values down or across, or down *and* across, as many cells as they require, and the formulas can be written anywhere in the worksheet besides.

But you could – for whatever reason – write the following (note the syntax):

=(@A1:A3*@B1:B3)

Again, those @ signs stand for the implicit intersection operator, which beat out this result depicted by Figure 9-3.

1	4	4 =(@A1:A3*@B1:B3)
2	5	
3	6	

Figure 9-3. *Holding back; this dynamic array formula yields one result*

We see that the operators constrain the formula to return but one result – the one situated on the row on which it's been written. Thus, Figure 9-4 illustrates the follow-on featuring precisely the same formula:

1	4	
2	5	10 =(@A1:A3*@B1:B3)
3	6	

Figure 9-4. *A comedown: once again, the formula only references the value on its row*

Another example is presented in Figure 9-5.

Today		
is		2 =SUM(LEN(@A1:A3))
Thursday		

Figure 9-5. *Going to great length: implicit intersection again forces one result*

And those results mimic what you'd see in a pre-365 edition of Excel.

All of which inspires the obvious question: when would I need to use this? The short answer: probably never.

After all, the likelihood you'd actually reach back for a feature that Excel has decided to overrule takes retro nostalgia a step too far. Several web-based discussions of the operator that I've seen suggest uses for the function that seem forced and contrived, as if their authors are similarly puzzled by the whole idea.

But in the interests of giving Microsoft the benefit of the doubt, allow me to spin a halfway plausible narrative in which the implicit intersection operator *might* be of service.

Where You Might Use the Intersect Operator – Maybe

Suppose you're teaching an online Excel class, only some of whose students have 365. In the course of your exposition of array formulas – which, given the variety of Excel versions resident in the students' machines, must be taught along two tracks – you want to demonstrate that formulas such as

=SUM(LEN(A1:A3))

can be written by all of the students, Excel version notwithstanding – provided of course that the pre-365 users bang out Ctrl-Shift-Enter to complete the formula.

But another contingency looms: what if a pre-365 user writes an array formula and *forgets* to strike Ctrl-Shift-Enter, pressing Enter instead – a mistake most easily committed?

What happens of course is implicit intersection. Write =SUM(LEN(A1:A3)) in a pre-365 version, tap Enter alone, and you get one value – *not* the sum of the lengths of the three words introduced in A1:A3, but again, the length of the word on the row in which you've composed the formula.

But remember *you*, the teacher, have Excel 365 under your hood, and so you *can't* recreate what's happening – because Excel 365 has eliminated implicit intersection.

And that's when you might turn to the implicit intersection operator, share your screen, and write

=SUM(LEN(@A1:A3))

Enter that expression and your formula will likewise return but one value. And as a consequence, you'll be able to confirm – and show – to the pre-365 user what result she'll see.

Thus, recourse to the implicit intersection operator in Excel 365 could serve a meaningful instructional purpose. But if teaching isn't your bag, the @ sign isn't where it's at.

They're Here, Probably: The Newest Dynamic Array Functions

But now we're going to begin to take a concerted look at some other functions that you probably *will* use – once you determine that they're there.

They're the newest batch of dynamic array functions – 14 in toto – that for the most part offer Excel users a number of enhancements to their customary ways of doing their work. Instead of dealing out an assortment of new means for number crunching, the new functions by and large issue a set of novel and important tools for organizing, and reorganizing, your datasets in ways that *facilitate* the crunching; and if that description is long on abstractions and short on examples, the examples will emerge in the ensuing chapters.

And yes, you should have the new functions now, pursuant to Microsoft's announcement on September 29, 2022 that "These functions are now fully deployed to Excel for the Web and users of Office 365 on the Current Channel".

And apropos the above, don't bother reconnoitering your inbox for a breathless, stop-the-presses email from Microsoft heralding the arrival of the functions – instead, they're just likely to show up one day, and you may not even know it until you type, or attempt to type, one of their names in a formula:

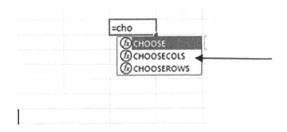

Figure 9-6. *Where did THEY come from?: CHOOSECOLS and CHOOSEROWS, two of the new dynamic array functions*

The new 14:

TEXT SPLIT

TEXT BEFORE

TEXTAFTER

TOCOL

TOROW

WRAPSOL

WRAPROWS

VSTACK

HSTACK

CHOOSECOLS

CHOOSEROWS

TAKE

DROP

EXPAND

can in fact be understood as a smaller set of groupings, because some address the organization of rows in a dataset, while others perform similar work on columns, and the like. And that means that acquainting yourself with the new set won't take quite so long as you may first assume – or fear.

Chapter 10 will kick off our review of the new functions by investigating the three that are designed to address – and solve – a batch of classic spreadsheet problems besetting the handling of text – TEXT SPLIT, TEXT BEFORE, and TEXT AFTER.

TEXTSPLIT, TEXTBEFORE, and TEXTAFTER: Putting Words in Their Places

Coming to a Hard Drive Near You

The three new dynamic array text functions take collective aim at a class of age-old and related spreadsheet problems – namely, how to separate, or parse, a cell containing a text string into its constituent words.

The prevailing instrument of choice for meeting that challenge was of course, and probably still is, the storied Text to Columns option, shown in Figure 10-1.

111

© Abbott Ira Katz 2023
A. I. Katz, *Up Up and Array!*, https://doi.org/10.1007/978-1-4842-8966-2_10

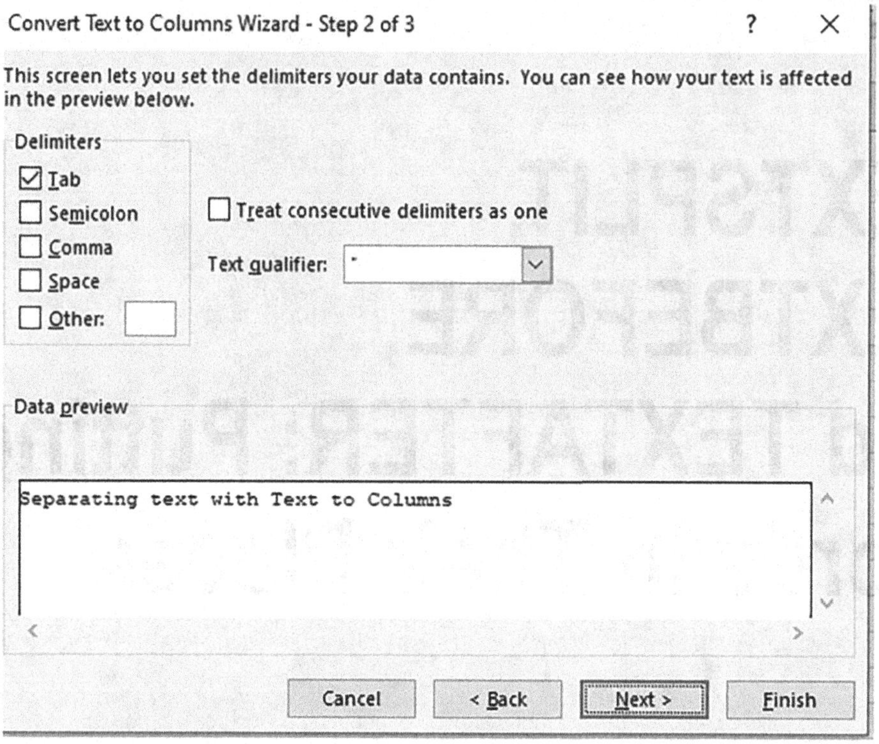

Figure 10-1. *Microsoft's words – assigning each word to a cell via Text to Columns*

Text to Columns works principally by enabling the user to define a *delimiter*, or delimiters, by which the text could be demarcated into a one-word-per-column motif. In the above shot the user would tick the "space" box, the character which would delimit the text into its respective words wherever it happened upon a space in the text entry.

In this regard, a classic application would be to ask Text to Columns to pull apart comma-separated values crammed into a single cell (e.g., the proverbial CSV file) into distinct *field* entries. For example, the New York Housing lottery spreadsheet with which we worked in Chapter 7 was in fact originally organized as a CSV file, with its header row looking like this in the excerpt supplied by Figure 10-2.

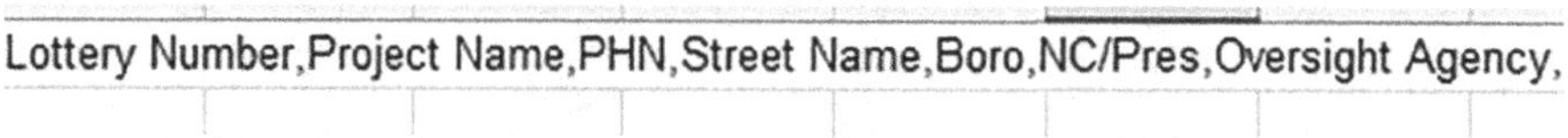

Lottery Number,Project Name,PHN,Street Name,Boro,NC/Pres,Oversight Agency,

Figure 10-2. *The great divide: a header row in CSV format before its field names have been separated*

Remember that all those budding headers (far more than you're actually viewing above) are jammed into a single cell, and Text to Columns would seize upon the delimiting commas and carve out a discrete a field name for each and every term hemmed in by those commas, and then proceed to do the same for all the comma-ridden rows beneath the headers as well, converting them all into field data.

Text to Columns has put in years of honorable service, but because it's click-based, its flexibility is stunted. For example, if I wanted to separate *and* sort the data – say, comma-separated test scores – Text to Columns would only perform the separation, but not the sort. Or if I needed to disentangle comma-separated values and *then* stack them vertically, again, you'd need to look elsewhere – in the direction of formulas.

And indeed – a number of formulaic means for parsing, or extracting, words or segments of text have long been made available, and we've already viewed some of them, for example, MID, LEFT, and SEARCH. But as this (https://www.linkedin.com/posts/andrewcharlesmoss_extracting-and-splitting-text-activity-6928128981799997440-NGpl/?utm_source=linkedin_share&utm_medium=member_desktop_web) piece notes, those strategies can get rather convoluted, and can stymie the user who's up against that quintessential text roadblock – separating first, middle, and last *names* that are all huddled in the same cell.

But help has arrived – in the form of three new, streamlining formulas that go a long way toward smoothing the bumps pockmarking the road to successful text separation – TEXTSPLIT, TEXTBEFORE, AND TEXTAFTER.

TEXTSPLIT: Piecing It Together

TEXTSPLIT carries out the most generic text separation of the three, liberating every delimited value in a text string to a cell all its own. Its six arguments look like this:

=TEXTSPLIT(text,column delimiter,row delimiter,ignore
empty,match mode,pad width)

As we'll see, the first two arguments – the one requiring you to identify the text you want to split and the one that names the delimiter(s) – are essential, while the remaining four offer themselves as options.

For example – say we enter "London is lovely this time of year" in a blank worksheet in B3. We can next write, in B6,

=TEXTSPLIT(B3," ")

And once you do, you should see the following, per Figure 10-3.

London is lovely this time of year						
=TEXTSPLIT(B3," ")						
London	is	lovely	this	time	of	year

Figure 10-3. *Spaced out: each word is assigned its own cell*

Here TEXTSPLIT searches our phrase for every *space*, the character we've nominated as the column delimiter. Each textual instance *preceding* a space is allotted its own cell, and as a result every word is properly separated, or split.

We see that this highly conventional deployment of TEXTSPLIT makes use of only two arguments – the text to be split, and the character earmarked as its column delimiter, for example, the character that will install each split item into a new column. Now if were we to write

=TEXTSPLIT(B3,," ")

we'd reengineer the outcome with this result, rendered by Figure 10-4.

London is lovely this time of year	
=TEXTSPLIT(B3,," ")	
London	
is	
lovely	
this	
time	
of	
year	

Figure 10-4. *London's text is falling down: TEXTSPLIT generates a vertical word split*

We've seen something like this before, for example, in our survey of the SEQUENCE function. The formula's additional comma bypasses the column delimiter argument and actuates a *row delimiter* instead – the space again, but which now acts as a kind of de facto line break, wrapping the split items down a column.

Now things get subtler, more interesting, and potentially more productive, when TEXTSPLIT is asked to incorporate both a column *and* a row delimiter into its expression. Consider this single-celled collection of student test scores, which you can enter in I5:

Ted 76,Jan 82,Mildred 91,Frank 64

Note how the cell's contents are organized: each score is distanced from its student by a space, while a comma demarcates the student name/scores from one another. If we write

=TEXTSPLIT(I5," ",",")

in cell I7, this happens, as we see in Figure 10-5.

Ted 76,Jan 82,Mildred 91,Frank 64	
=TEXTSPLIT(I5," ",",")	
Ted	76
Jan	82
Mildred	91
Frank	64

Figure 10-5. *Every which way; the text is split both across and down a column*

The space delimiter spills each student name/score downwards, while at the same time the comma neatly pairs each name and its corresponding score horizontally. Just remember to line up all those quotation marks properly.

Note   The test scores returned above by TEXTSPLIT nevertheless have the status of *text* (note their left alignment). There are ways of treating these as numeric values, though, for example, through the VALUE function.

In effect we've compiled a mini data set of names and scores, which now can be further manipulated, for example,

=SORT(TEXTSPLIT(I5," ",","),2,-1)

yielding the following, as you see in Figure 10-6.

Ted 76,Jan 82,Mildred 91,Frank 64	
=SORT(TEXTSPLIT(I5," ",","),2,-1)	
Mildred	91
Jan	82
Ted	76
Frank	64

Figure 10-6. *Sorting the scoring in a single cell*

(Note again that Excel allows the sort to proceed, even though the scores are officially text-formatted.)

There'll be more to be said about TEXTSPLIT's coupling of column and row delimiters a bit later.

Choose Your Delimiters

But who insisted that the space character serve as TEXTSPLIT's only delimiter? No one, in fact. The reality is that you can invest *any* character – or characters – with delimiter status.

For example, observe this phrase:

We wanted to go out, but it was raining. What was Plan B?

A number of different characters – period, comma, and question mark, along with the space – are clinging to the words to be separated, but if were we to decide that the space *alone* was to delimit them, the results would look like this according to Figure 10-7.

We	wanted	to	go	out,	but	it	was	raining.	What	was	Plan	B?

Figure 10-7. *Spreadsheet grammar – unwanted punctuation*

But we want to authorize *all* the above characters – period, comma, question mark, and space – to delimit words, rather than loiter idly among them, as they do in the screen shot. How do we do that?

Here's how Microsoft wants you to do it, and the syntax isn't pretty:

$$=TEXTSPLIT(E8,\{" ",",",".","?"\},,1)$$

Got that? Still squinting, or have you given up? If so, sit back and consider this explanation: first, all the designated delimiters are bounded by a familiar pair of user-typed array-formula brackets. And inside, each delimiter is in turn enclosed by quotes and detached from the next delimiter by a comma – remembering at the same time that one of the delimiters *itself* is a comma, and is thus sandwiched between two of the quotes.

Is all that syntax hard to read and user-friendly? Yes and no. Of course, it works, once you coordinate all those quotes and commas; but there's a more lucid equivalent out there about which you want to know.

For an alternative means for citing multi-delimiters, enter all the desired delimiters down a column. Here, none of these should be surrounded by quotes. For the space delimiter, simply type a space in its cell. Then remake the column into a table via Ctrl-T, and don't worry about a formal table header, as Figure 10-8 demonstrates.

Figure 10-8. *Delimiters, quote-free. The invisible space delimiter occupies the first table cell.*

The table of course assumes the default Table1 name, facilitating this TEXTSPLIT rewrite

=TEXTSPLIT(E8,Table1,,1)

The Table1 reference serves as a proxy for the bracketed, quote-thickened delimiters, and performs in precisely the same way. Moreover, if it turns out that you need more delimiters or remember ones you'd omitted, simply enter them down the table column, and they too will automatically split any words. It's a rather cool, far neater substitute for the official, by-the-book, bracketed delimiter argument.

You Won't Always Ignore "Ignore Empty"

But if you travel the table route mapped above, you'll need to make sure that TEXTSPLIT's fourth, optional "ignore empty" argument finds a place in the formula, as we see it represented above by the 1. "Ignore empty" instructs the function to disregard a delimiter that's unaccompanied by any text to be split – and if you overlook it, the formula we've detailed will inflict unnecessary spaces upon the results. For example, without "ignore empty," the *space* following the word "out," will populate a cell all its own – because the comma alongside "out" will have *already* delimited that word, and the space will then be treated as an empty delimiter.

By way of additional example, if the name Ted above in our earlier student-grades formula had been mistakenly exhibited *two* following spaces instead of one, our original TEXTSPLIT expression (excluding the "ignore empty" argument) would have inflicted this result upon the worksheet, exemplified by Figure 10-9.

Ted 76,Jan 82,Mildred 91,Frank 64		
=TEXTSPLIT(I5," ",",")		
Ted		76
Jan	82	#N/A
Mildred	91	#N/A
Frank	64	#N/A

Figure 10-9.. *Outer space – Ted is separated from his test score by two spaces*

We see that by default, superfluous delimiters are *not* ignored, and as such the result above makes room for *both* of Ted's spaces – the first delimiting nothing, the second, the 76. And because that surplus space – which is, after all, a column delimiter – pushes Ted's score into a new, extra, third column; that column is now imposed upon the other names, too, forcing them to emit a #N/A error message. You can't earmark a new column for only one row, after all; it's an all-or-nothing proposition. Ted's row can't receive three columns even as the other names hold to the original two.

The workaround: editing the formula to read

=TEXTSPLIT(I5," ",",",1)

where the "1" issues an "ignore empty cells" order, the results return to a two-columned, error-free outcome.

Note   Wrapping the TRIM function around formulas will eliminate superfluous spaces from a text string.

Note that there may be standard data-management scenarios under which you *don't* want the TEXTSPLIT formula to ignore an empty delimiter, for example, this simple example in Figure 10-10.

Name,id,score
Bill,,67
Jane,187,92
Ed,246,78

Figure 10-10. *Where's your ID, Bill?*

Here, you'll *want* Bill's missing ID to be taken into account, because when the data are eventually split you'll want to see this, per Figure 10-11.

Name	id	score
Bill		67
Jane	187	92
Ed	246	78

Figure 10-11. *These fields are lined up*

and not this, as presented in Figure 10-12.

Name	id	score
Bill	67	
Jane	187	92
Ed	246	78

Figure 10-12. *These fields aren't*

We see that if you *do* ignore the empty delimiter via the 1 argument, TEXTSPLIT will throw Bill's next-available bit of data – 67, a test score – into the next available column, id; and as you see, that decision misaligns the data from their appropriate columns. Thus, we see that the first of Bill's two consecutive commas supplies a placeholder for a field – id – for which information is missing. (We'll have more to say about this example, too.)

The fifth argument – match mode – points to case-sensitivity, which is turned *on* by default. For example, this expression

TodayXisXThursday

has for some reason appointed X to the delimiter role. If we write

=TEXTSPLIT(G12,"x")

Figure 10-13 discloses what happens next.

| =TEXTSPLIT(G12,"x") |
| TodayXisXThursday |

Figure 10-13. *Curious case: no change*

Nothing happens, in fact, because TEXSPLIT's default case-sensitivity ignores and thus looks past the capital X. Write this, however:

=TEXTSPLIT(G12,"x",,,1)

where the 1 switches the case-insensitive option *on*, and Figure 10-14 confirms.

| =TEXTSPLIT(G12,"x",,,1) | | |
| today | is | thursday |

Figure 10-14. *x marks the split: the text is split by TEXTSPLIT*

Launching "Pad With": A New Kind of Argument

The utility of the sixth TEXTSPLIT argument – what Excel calls "pad with" – was already implied in a previous exercise. "Pad with" – a parameter option that appears in many of the new dynamic array functions – is a user-selected character or characters that replace any error messages that could beset a formula. Thus the #NA errors triggered by Ted's extra space depicted by Figure 10-9 could be preempted by a "Not Available" pad, for example, Figure 10-15.

Ted 76,Jan 82,Mildred 91,Frank 64		
=TEXTSPLIT(I5," ",",",,"Not Available")		
Ted		76
Jan	82	Not Available
Mildred	91	Not Available
Frank	64	Not Available

Figure 10-15. *Scouring pad: the "pad with" option cleans up error messages.*

One could ask why Excel felt the need to coin the term "pad width," one that doesn't appear in any of the pre-dynamic array functions. After all, other functions, for example, XLOOKUP and FILTER, offer "if not found" or "if empty" arguments that *also* allow the user to post a replacement caption for formulas that would otherwise succumb to error messages. But isn't that what "pad with" does, too? And if so, why did the folks at Microsoft's usability team need to mint a new term for this feature that seems to do much the same as its predecessors?

The answer is that Excel *could* have fallen back on an existing term such as "if not found" here, but "pad with" makes a statement about the different kind of work that some of the new dynamic array functions perform. When a user performs a query with FILTER, for example, the number of results churned out by the formula will vary, depending on the filter criteria the user employs; but functions such as TEXTSPLIT and, as we'll see, WRAPCOLS and EXPAND, ask the user to frame a spill range of *fixed size* at the *outset*, for example, three rows by four columns; and because some of those cells may, for whatever reason, be blank, the user is granted the option to fill out – or pad – the bare cells with a caption.

TEXTSPLIT and the One-Celled Dataset

Earlier in this chapter we looked at a few hypothetical exam scores and the names of the students who scored them, as a means of demonstrating TEXTSPLIT's talent for cracking open the data gathered into one cell into both columnar and row entries, for example, in Figure 10-16.

Ted 76,Jan 82,Mildred 91,Frank 64		
=TEXTSPLIT(I5," ",",")		
Ted	76	
Jan	82	
Mildred	91	
Frank	64	

Figure 10-16. *Look familiar? TEXTSPLIT test splits*

But now let's flip the matter on its head. We've seen that TEXTSPLIT can unpack a collection of data concentrated in one cell, and distribute, or split, them into multiple, usable cells. With that skill in tow, why can't we take existing data, repack them into a single cell via the TEXTJOIN function, and then call them back into conventional cell-based entries when we want to? In other words, why not compress and store records into one cell – even a few thousand records – and empty the cell into distinct records again whenever we need them with TEXTSPLIT?

To illustrate the strategy, I've drawn 100 unique student first names from the list of US Congresspersons we encountered in the chapter on FILTER and associated them with randomly issued test scores (enabled by RANDARRAY, of course), and saved to the *TEXTSPLIT - test scores* practice file (with range names Student and Score). As advertised, we want to concatenate all the names and scores into *one* cell under the auspices of this TEXTJOIN formula:

=TEXTJOIN("*",,,Student&","&Score)

TEXTJOIN is a surprisingly handy and muscular function that can combine, or concatenate, multiple cells' worth of text via a delimiter. Here, TEXTJOIN merges every student name and test score in a pairwise-lifted tandem, punctuated by a comma that's interposed between each name-score pair. That is, each name is joined to its score, for example, Smith, 78. But it's the *asterisk* that's serving as a delimiter, for reasons that'll become much clearer in a moment. (The two consecutive commas in the formula point to TEXTJOIN's "ignore empty" option which isn't pertinent here; our data contain no empty cells.)

Write that formula, say in D4, and in excerpt you should see, as per Figure 10-17.

```
=TEXTJOIN("*",,Student&","&Score)
Abby,61*Abigail,70*Adam,66*Adrian,62*Adriano,49*Al,43*Alan,36*Albio,70*,
```

Figure 10-17. *Big class: 100 students and their scores, all joined in D4*

(Now you can run a Copy > Paste Values atop D4.)

Note what the data currently look like. Each student name is followed by the test score on the other side of the comma. But each name/score is in turn separated from the *next* name/score by that asterisk – the delimiter we selected for TEXTJOIN. And now what?

How about TEXTSPLIT?

$$=TEXTSPLIT(D4,",","*")$$

which delivers the following, as excerpted by Figure 10-18.

=TEXTSPLIT(D4,",","*")	
Abby	61
Abigail	70
Adam	66
Adrian	62
Adriano	49
Al	43
Alan	36
Albio	70
Alcee	96
Alexander	77
Alexandria	76
Alma	70
Ami	41
Andy	48
Angie	42
Ann	53
Anna	80
Anthony	71

Figure 10-18. *The dataset, returned in full: names and test scores unlocked from D4 and reassigned to separate cells*

Again, TEXTSPLIT splits the data in two directions: it seizes upon the comma column delimiter – grabbed from TEXTJOIN's concatenation comma – to segregate the student names from their scores, and *also* applies TEXTJOIN's own, official delimiter, the asterisk, to swing each record down to the next row by citing the asterisk in its "row delimiter" argument.

The larger point: TEXTSPLIT can skillfully break comma-separated values into functional data, but you can point that process in the other direction – retroactively define standard, separated data as a cohort of comma-separated values saved to one cell, and *then* recreate the dataset on an as needed-basis via TEXTSPLIT. That is, have TEXTJOIN round up hundreds or perhaps even thousands of records into one cell (remember an Excel cell can hold 32,767 characters) and retrieve them with TEXTSPLIT when you want to.

TEXTSPLIT Can't Do Everything – but with Good Reason

Yet for all of TEXTSPLIT's admirable dexterity, there's one text manipulation chore it can't quite perform. TEXTSPLIT is unable to split multiple rows of text directly with a single application of its formula – meaning that, for example, if you're working with three text-bearing cells, say in C7:C9 and Figure 10-19,

Today is Thursday	
My favorite flavor is Rocky Road	
Annapolis is the capital of Maryland	

Figure 10-19. *Three cells to be split*

you can't write

$$=TEXTSPLIT(C7:C9, " ")$$

And if you do, you'll achieve the following, per Figure 10-20.

| Today is Thursday |
| My favorite flavor is Rocky Road |
| Annapolis is the capital of Maryland |
| |
| |
| =TEXTSPLIT(C7:C9," ") |
| Today |
| My |
| Annapolis |

Figure 10-20. *You can't get there from here: TEXTSPLIT can't split all the text from the three cells referenced by one formula.*

We see that when confronted with a range of cells named by a single formula, each of which requires splitting, TEXTSPLIT will only split the first word from each cell. Thus, if you need an authentic, thoroughgoing word split applied to each cell, each cell requires its own TEXTSPLIT formula, for example, in Figure 10-21.

Today is Thursday	Today	is	Thursday				=TEXTSPLIT(C7," ")
My favorite flavor is Rocky Road	My	favorite	flavor	is	Rocky	Road	=TEXTSPLIT(C8," ")
Annapolis is the capital of Maryland	Annapolis	is	the	capital	of	Maryland	=TEXTSPLIT(C9," ")

Figure 10-21. *Splitting text, one line and one formula at a time*

Indeed, our earlier illustration in this chapter of the "ignore empty" argument that was applied to the following data and as recalled in Figure 10-22:

| Name,id,score |
| Bill,,67 |
| Jane,187,92 |
| Ed,246,78 |

Figure 10-22. *No teacher's pets: every student receives a TEXTSPLIT formula*

Split the text via three TEXTSPLIT formulas, one each per row.

However, keep in mind that Google Sheet's SPLIT function *can* cull the text from multiple cells with a single formula, as in Figure 10-23.

Today is Thursday					
My favorite flavor is Rocky Road					
Annapolis is the capital of Maryland					
=ArrayFormula(SPLIT(D7:D9," "))					
Today	is	Thursday			
My	favorite	flavor	is	Rocky	Road
Annapolis	is	the	capital	of	Maryland

Figure 10-23. *Message from the competition: Google Sheets' SPLIT function can split text in multiple cells with one formula*

Why, then, can't TEXSPLIT do the same?

One apparent reason why a single instance of TEXTSPLIT can't split multiple cells of text has to do with its two-dimensional potential. We've seen that TEXTSPLIT can implement both column *and* row delimiters, the latter of which generates multiple rows of text down a column. In that light, reconsider our formula:

$$=TEXTSPLIT(C7:C9, " ")$$

We see now that if the text in C7 were subjected to a row delimiter and hence spilled its words down the C column, its output would bump against and be obstructed by the text in C8, the next row down, and TEXTSPLIT can't resolve that logjam. On the other hand, Google Sheet's SPLIT function won't be bothered by that complication – because it has no row delimiter to begin with.

There Is a Plan B

But a workaround is available, one suggested by the one-cell dataset exercise above. If you try

$$=TEXTSPLIT(TEXTJOIN("*",,C7:C9)," ","*",,,"")$$

that expression would yield as follows, as featured in Figure 10-24.

Today is Thursday					
My favorite flavor is Rocky Road					
Annapolis is the capital of Maryland					
=TEXTSPLIT(TEXTJOIN("*",,C7:C9)," ","*",,,"")					
Today	is	Thursday			
My	favorite	flavor	is	Rocky	Road
Annapolis	is	the	capital	of	Maryland

Figure 10-24. *Breaking up isn't that hard to do: the three text strings are knit together in one cell by TEXTJOIN, and then split into words with TEXTSPLIT*

The linchpin to the formula is TEXTJOIN's ability to stitch the three strings into a *single cell*, thus forging in effect one large text string. And that's precisely the kind of object TEXTSPLIT is designed to handle – one text string in one cell. Thus, if we isolate the TEXTJOIN portion of the formula, we'll see

Today is Thursday*My favorite flavor is Rocky Road*Annapolis is the capital of Maryland

And as with the earlier one-celled dataset example, TEXTJOIN registers the asterisk as its delimiter, which TEXTSPLIT in turn borrows for its own *row* delimiter, thus splitting the string back to its original three rows of text. TEXTSPLIT's column delimiter – here the space – then divides each string into discrete words.

The formula's final pair of quotes, the ones shunted to the far-right end of the formula, expresses the "pad with" argument. They're needed here because the first text string – Today is Thursday – comprises just three words extending across three columns, while the other two strings and their six words naturally span six. And as explained earlier in the chapter, since "Today is Thursday" must also be afforded six columns – because every row in the spill range must exhibit the same number of columns – its three empty cells default to an #N/A message that can be overwritten with a "pad with" caption.

TEXTBEFORE and TEXTAFTER: Usefully Limiting the Delimiters

Cousins to the broader, more generic TEXTSPLIT, the new TEXTBEFORE and TEXTAFTER dynamic array functions offer a slightly narrower approach to the work of isolating specific text from cells, but presumably with a famed – or notorious – task specifically in mind, one to which we've already alluded.

That task: Taking full names crowded into a single cell and splitting them into first, middle, and last names – and TEXTBEFORE and TEXTAFTER stand ready to offer their able assistance. TEXTBEFORE returns text that appears *before* a specified instance of a delimiter, while TEXTAFTER travels in the opposite direction – it carries off text that *follows* a specified delimiter instance.

How They're Written – and How They Work

As you might infer, the two functions are written similarly and feature a number of subtle arguments you'll need to consider. TEXTBEFORE assumes this form:

> =TEXTBEFORE(text,delimiter(s),instance number,match mode,match end,if not found)

The first argument asks you to furnish the address of the text in question, though of course it's perfectly legal to actually type the text into the formula, for example, =TEXTBEFORE("John Doe"," "). As with TEXTSPLIT the formula needs to know the delimiter(s) of choice, which can indeed consist of several possibilities, and which would be entered as they are with TEXTSPLIT, for example,

> {" ","*"}

And again, you can refer the delimiters to a table instead and supply the table name as a global delimiter name(s) in the formula.

The third argument, instance number, is central to the process. The number refers to the sequence position of a particular delimiter among all the delimiters in the cell. Simple example: the space delimiter preceding Sartre in the name John Paul Sartre is the *second* space in the cell proceeding from left to right, and as such would be designated 2 in TEXTBEFORE.

However, you can also note the instance number with a *negative* value, an option that initiates the delimiter count from the *right* end of the text and proceeds left, thus requiring a bit of a think-through. Working this way, that second space before Sartre would be coded -1 – meaning in this case that the space is the *first* delimiter in the cell pointing right to left. -2 in the same formula, then, would denote the *second* delimiter per the right-to-left orientation – and here, that would point to the space separating Jean and Paul. It sounds a bit obtuse, but as we'll see, that reverse numbering scheme can serve you well.

And if you omit instance number altogether, TEXTBEFORE will work with the delimiter's first instance by default.

The next argument, match mode, behaves similarly to its counterpart in TEXTSPLIT. As with that function, TEXTBEFORE turns its case-sensitivity on, such that addressing the text string

TodayXisXThursday

with

=TEXTBEFORE(L14,"x")

(The other omitted arguments are optional.)

will trigger an #N/A message. This will work, though, as it deactivates case-sensitivity:

=TEXTBEFORE(L14,"x",,1)

Now apart from sounding like the conclusion of a sporting event, the fifth argument, "match end," is trickier but can be put to productive use once you appreciate exactly what it does – something that took me a while. Inactive by default and denoted by the value 1 when it's used, Microsoft says that "match end" "Treats the end of text as a delimiter," a description that for me, at least, didn't little to advance my understanding.

But here's what that means in practical terms: match end in effect makes a copy of your delimiter (or one of your delimiters, if you've designated several) and appends it to the end of the text string, immediately following its last character. Thus, if the final character in your string is a "y," as in Today is Thursday, and your chosen delimiter is the space, match end will now treat the string as if it reads

Today is Thursday[space]

And now that Excel has outfitted the string with the delimiter, TEXTBEFORE and TEXTAFTER can find it, and act upon it.

Here's a relatively straightforward example of how match end works: say you're faced with a range of names from which you need to elicit the first names. If Tom Jones is niched in cell A3, this formula

=TEXTBEFORE(A3," ")

will naturally return Tom. But what if the name Madonna follows in A4? That entry as it stands features no space, and so TEXTBEFORE will default to an error message when it's applied to the cell. But this expression

=TEXTBEFORE(A4," ",,,1)

will station its virtual delimiter after the second "a" in Madonna. In effect, now, the formula will read Madonna as Madonna[space], and return all the text preceding that insurgent space – that is, Madonna.

TEXTBEFORE's final argument, "if not found," again lets the user again supply a message that subs for the #N/A that would otherwise appear if the delimiter was completely absent from the text string. Figure 10-25 should be pretty self-explanatory.

Today is Thursday	
Missing	=TEXTBEFORE(G8,"X",2,,,"Missing")

Figure 10-25. *Attendance report: X is marked absent*

TEXTAFTER: The Flip Side of TEXTBEFORE

TEXTAFTER, in effect a mirror image of TEXTBEFORE, sports the same syntax – with the essential distinction that the delimiter argument here seeks text that *follows* the appearance of the delimiter. Thus, for the space-delimited name John Doe, TEXTBEFORE will extract John – the name preceding the space, while TEXTAFTER will scrape the Doe, the text positioned after the space.

By way of a hands-on demo, let's open the *TEXTBEFORE and TEXTAFTER* practice workbook and its catalog of ten names as listed in Figure 10-26.

Angelina Jolie
Emily Dickinson
George Clooney
John Paul Sartre
LeBron James
Meryl Streep
Michael Jordan
Mick Jagger
Ricky Lee Jones
Sandra Bullock

Figure 10-26. *The A-list*

Our assignment here, a common one: to separate first from last names, while at the same time deciding where to position those thorny *middle* names that have been known to bedevil rosters and invitation lists.

Now in fact formula-based strategies for lifting first names from multi-name entries have long been in circulation, tying themselves to the LEFT and FIND functions. But TEXTS BEFORE and TEXTAFTER have some more lucid and elegant tricks up their sleeve, as we'll see.

By way of an introductory run-through, say we want to split the names into two columns – the first to record the first names, the second reserved for the remaining names, be they last name or middle/last name in combination. In cell B1 enter

=TEXT BEFORE(A1:A10," ")

But wait. Didn't we just learn just a few pages ago that a TEXTSPLIT formula was incapable of splitting text from *multiple cells*' worth of data? We sure did. But TEXTS BEFORE and TEXTAFTER don't suffer from that limitation. The absence of a row delimiter in TEXT BEFORE and TEXTAFTER means that they'll never spill *down* and encroach upon the text in the cell beneath it – unlike TEXSPLIT.

That important digression aside, remember that by *not* specifying a delimiter number we've in effect asked TEXT BEFORE to home in on the first instance of a space by default, and do its parsing wherever it's found – and so we see as follows, per Figure 10-27.

Angelina Jolie	Angelina	=TEXTBEFORE(A1:A10," ")
Emily Dickinson	Emily	
George Clooney	George	
John Paul Sartre	John	
LeBron James	LeBron	
Meryl Streep	Meryl	
Michael Jordan	Michael	
Mick Jagger	Mick	
Ricky Lee Jones	Ricky	
Sandra Bullock	Sandra	

Figure 10-27. *Celebrities, on a first-name basis*

That works. Now for the remaining names, enter in C1

$$=TEXTAFTER(A1:A10," ")$$

yielding the following, in Figure 10-28.

Angelina Jolie	Angelina	Jolie	=TEXTAFTER(A1:A10," ")
Emily Dickinson	Emily	Dickinson	
George Clooney	George	Clooney	
John Paul Sartre	John	Paul Sartre	
LeBron James	LeBron	James	
Meryl Streep	Meryl	Streep	
Michael Jordan	Michael	Jordan	
Mick Jagger	Mick	Jagger	
Ricky Lee Jones	Ricky	Lee Jones	
Sandra Bullock	Sandra	Bullock	

Figure 10-28. *Big Sur: surnames via TEXT AFTER*

Here by default TEXT AFTER sights the first space in each respective name, and fills each cell with all the text to the space's *right*.

That's all pretty neat and tidy – and by way of contrast if you were to try TEXT SPLIT for the above exercise instead, recall first of all that you'd require a new formula for each and every name – so if you went ahead, you'd get the following, as in Figure 10-29.

Angelina	Jolie		=TEXTSPLIT(A1," ")
Emily	Dickinson		=TEXTSPLIT(A2," ")
George	Clooney		=TEXTSPLIT(A3," ")
John	Paul	Sartre	=TEXTSPLIT(A4," ")
LeBron	James		=TEXTSPLIT(A5," ")
Meryl	Streep		=TEXTSPLIT(A6," ")
Michael	Jordan		=TEXTSPLIT(A7," ")
Mick	Jagger		=TEXTSPLIT(A8," ")
Ricky	Lee	Jones	=TEXTSPLIT(A9," ")
Sandra	Bullock		=TEXTSPLIT(A10," ")

Figure 10-29. *Having second thoughts about second names? Splitting names with TEXTSPLIT*

Probably not what you had in mind – because while TEXTSPLIT manages to split each and every name, the two middle names share column B with most of the surnames.

Front and Center: Extracting Middle Names

So what if you also wanted to isolate middle names, and then direct them properly to a dedicated column too, as per Figure 10-30?

Angelina Jolie	Angelina		Jolie
Emily Dickinson	Emily		Dickinson
George Clooney	George		Clooney
John Paul Sartre	John	Paul	Sartre
LeBron James	LeBron		James
Meryl Streep	Meryl		Streep
Michael Jordan	Michael		Jordan
Mick Jagger	Mick		Jagger
Ricky Lee Jones	Ricky	Lee	Jones
Sandra Bullock	Sandra		Bullock

Figure 10-30. *Caught in the middle: middle names captured as well*

That ambition is a little grander, because the TEXT BEFORE/AFTER functions spirit away *all* of the text on either side of a delimiter. But here we want to glean text wedged *between* two delimiters, surrounded by unwanted text on either side.

In order to carry out that mission we'll have to execute *two* text extractions, and nest one text expression inside another. First, we'll move the last names we induced in an earlier exercise from the C to the D column, and then write in C1

=TEXTAFTER(TEXT BEFORE(A1:A10," ",-1)," ",,,1)

Of course, the juxtaposing of both TEXTAFTER and TEXT BEFORE in the same formula needs to be explained. Working from the inside out, the TEXTBEFORE segment acts upon the first space delimiter appearing in each name from the name's *right* edge, as represented by the negative number. Thus, the TEXT BEFORE portion considered by itself would yield the following, as in Figure 10-31.

Angelina	=TEXTBEFORE(A1:A10," ",-1)
Emily	
George	
John Paul	
LeBron	
Meryl	
Michael	
Mick	
Ricky Lee	
Sandra	

Figure 10-31. *The right stuff: text returned from left of the rightmost space in each name*

Of course these are mid-way results, forming a temporary, virtual dataset that supplies names – each of which now features, or will feature, but one space – upon which the TEXT AFTER half of the formula is about to act.

And when we wrap TEXT AFTER around TEXTBEFORE, the formula now examines the names pictured above and simply yanks the text *following* the one and only space remaining within each name. In the case of John Paul, then, the name Paul is returned; in the case of the cells bearing only one name, again the "match end" delimiter latches its faux space to the end of the name – and TEXTAFTER discovers nothing after it, leaving the cell blank.

Sorting Last Names: Sort of Tricky

Now what if you wanted to sort the data by last names – even if the cells to be sorted contain the names in full? In order to follow through on that slightly challenging intention you need first to decide if you want middle names to figure in the sort – that is, to be sorted themselves (e.g., the P in John Paul Sartre). If not – that is, if you want to sort exclusively by last, or surname – you could write

=SORTBY(A1:A10,TEXTAFTER(A1:A10," ",-1))

And that formula spills, shown by Figure 10-32.

Angelina Jolie	Sandra Bullock	=SORTBY(A1:A10,TEXTAFTER(A1:A10," ",-1))
Emily Dickinson	George Clooney	
George Clooney	Emily Dickinson	
John Paul Sartre	Mick Jagger	
LeBron James	LeBron James	
Meryl Streep	Angelina Jolie	
Michael Jordan	Ricky Lee Jones	
Mick Jagger	Michael Jordan	
Ricky Lee Jones	John Paul Sartre	
Sandra Bullock	Meryl Streep	

Figure 10-32. *Internal alphabetical order: sorting by last names*

How does this formula work? We want the A1:A10 range to be subjected to a sort-by range (i.e., the formula's second argument) consisting of the *last names only* derived by TEXTAFTER, which line up in turn with the full names enumerated in A1:A10 (proffered by the formula's first argument). That is, the formula achieves the last-name sort *internally*, as you see in Figure 10-33 but *won't* see in the actual spreadsheet.

Angelina Jolie	Jolie	=TEXTAFTER(A1:A10," ",-1)
Emily Dickinson	Dickinson	
George Clooney	Clooney	
John Paul Sartre	Sartre	
LeBron James	James	
Meryl Streep	Streep	
Michael Jordan	Jordan	
Mick Jagger	Jagger	
Ricky Lee Jones	Jones	
Sandra Bullock	Bullock	

Figure 10-33. *Behind the scenes: this part of the formula sorts last names only*

It then proceeds in effect to sort the two columns – that is, the actual data in A and the virtual column of last names returned inside the formula – by the latter, which brings the first-column names, the ones we actually view in the worksheet along for the ride.

Some Concluding Words

Number crunching may be Excel's stock in trade, but as we've seen there's plenty of work it can do with words, too; and the new text functions strive to make that work simpler and more productive.

The next pair of new dynamic array functions, TOCOL and TOROW, flattens multi-column or multi-row ranges into a single column or row. And you'll see why you'll want to add these new terms to your spreadsheet vocabulary.

CHAPTER 11

TOCOL and TOROW: Straightening Out the Data

To reiterate an introductory point we made a short while ago: Excel's new, second-generation dynamic array functions don't open many new windows on number crunching; rather, they're primarily about revamping and streamlining the way in which data can be *organized*. And that's a point that surely calls for some explanation, beginning with a description of the TOROW and TOCOL functions.

How They're Written – and What They're About

TOCOL and TOROW were crafted to allow users simpler means for analyzing data that's currently committed to a rectangular form. So what does that mean?

Try this example on for size. Suppose you're faced with a collection of numbers occupying a range of 12 rows and 5 columns in G6:J17 (practice file: *TOCOL – number matrix*), its integers ranging in value from one through ten, per Figure 11-1.

© Abbott Ira Katz 2023
A. I. Katz, *Up Up and Array!*, https://doi.org/10.1007/978-1-4842-8966-2_11

1	3	9	7
2	5	6	3
3	4	8	7
9	2	3	4
5	3	3	8
10	4	7	3
3	6	1	2
4	9	2	9
5	1	7	2
4	2	9	3
5	1	5	9
9	10	1	4

Figure 11-1. *The matrix: the sequel*

We want to count the frequency with which each value appears in the range, but the dispersion of those values across five columns makes the exercise something of a pause giver – because before we can count each value with the standard COUNTIF function we need to list each value uniquely as criteria, so that COUNTIF knows what it's counting; and assembling a unique list of values across columns is no straightforward thing.

Enter TOCOL, which is happy to throw itself at multi-column data and distill them all into a *single* column, after which all kinds of data-analytic tasks become much easier. After all, once you've somehow squeezed all the above values into one column – even temporarily – the UNIQUE function can fearlessly spring into action.

TOCOL (note that its name is phrased in the singular) exhibits three arguments, only one of which is absolutely required:

=TOCOL(range/array,ignore,scan by column)

The first argument, range, or what Excel again terms "array," simply requests the coordinates of the data with which TOCOL is to work – that is, which data will be reshaped into a single column.

The second argument, "ignore," presents itself as an option but can be surprisingly useful, as we'll see. Ignore accepts four possible arguments expressed as values 1 through 4 in Figure 11-2.

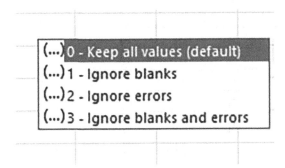

Figure 11-2. *TOCOL ignore options; don't ignore them*

The first as conveyed by the 0, Keep all values, serves as the default option and can be omitted; it simply preserves all existing values in the range/array and will return them all to the single column TOCOL will construct. Ignore blanks does just that, that is, it forsakes any empty cells in the source range/array and bars them from the TOCOL result, and ignore errors does the same for error-message-bearing cells. The fourth option, ignore blanks and errors, combines the operations of options 2 and 3.

The optional "scan by column" argument is also handier than you may initially suspect, and to demonstrate what it does let's first write

=TOCOL(G6:J27)

in its option-free default mode, in cell L6. You should see (in excerpt) as in Figure 11-3.

				=TOCOL(G6:J17)
1	3	9	7	1
2	5	6	3	3
3	4	8	7	9
9	2	3	4	7
5	3	3	8	2
10	4	7	3	5
3	6	1	2	6
4	9	2	9	3
5	1	7	2	3
4	2	9	3	4
5	1	5	9	8
9	10	1	4	7
				9
				2

Figure 11-3. *All four one – the matrix narrowed to a single column*

You'll note the first four values populating the spill range – 1, 3, 9, and 7 – reference the entries in the matrix' first row, with 2, 5, 6, 3, reflecting the values in row two, etc. If, however, we edit our formula to read

=TOCOL(G6:J17,,1)

where the 1 embodies what's called the "scan by column" option, the results get flipped, per Figure 11-4.

				=TOCOL(G6:J17,,1)
1	3	9	7	1
2	5	6	3	2
3	4	8	7	3
9	2	3	4	9
5	3	3	8	5
10	4	7	3	10
3	6	1	2	3
4	9	2	9	4
5	1	7	2	5
4	2	9	3	4
5	1	5	9	5
9	10	1	4	9
				3
				5

Figure 11-4. Heading in a different direction: the results dive down the columns for their results

Here, the first four TOCOL results capture the 1, 2, 3, and 9 from the matrix' first *column,* because the values are searched downwards.

But let's not lose sight of our wider aim: we want to count the number of times each value appears in the matrix – and so we can remake our formula per that intent, and realize these outcomes, presented in Figure 11-5.

=SORT(UNIQUE(TOCOL(G6:J17,,1)))

1	3	9	7		1
2	5	6	3		2
3	4	8	7		3
9	2	3	4		4
5	3	3	8		5
10	4	7	3		6
3	6	1	2		7
4	9	2	9		8
5	1	7	2		9
4	2	9	3		10
5	1	5	9		
9	10	1	4		

Figure 11-5. *Each matrix value – once each, in numerical order*

Now that we've uniquely enumerated the matrix' values, we can add this expression to M6:

$$=COUNTIF(G6:J17,L6\#)$$

yielding in turn the following, in Figure 11-6.

=SORT(UNIQUE(TOCOL(G6:J17,,1)))

1	3	9	7		1	5 =COUNTIF(G6:J17,L6#)
2	5	6	3		2	6
3	4	8	7		3	9
9	2	3	4		4	6
5	3	3	8		5	5
10	4	7	3		6	2
3	6	1	2		7	4
4	9	2	9		8	2
5	1	7	2		9	7
4	2	9	3		10	2
5	1	5	9			
9	10	1	4			

Figure 11-6. *Matrix values, ac-counted for*

Mission accomplished. We've brought the TOCOL function to bear on multi-column data, thus enabling us to easily collect unique instances of each value.

Now what if we wanted to *sort* the matrix values – *within the multi-columned matrix*? That's also something we can do, but that assignment awaits the next chapter, in which we debut the WRAPCOLS and WRAPROWS functions and partner them with TOCOL

Drawing a Bead on the Blanks

In view of the kinds of work that TOCOL and/or TOROW can perform, a face-to-face showdown with some nasty blank cells just might be in the offing. In that light consider this practice worksheet (file: *TOCOL – attendance*), in which the presence of ten hypothetical students has been recorded in A2:E11 (row 1 has been reserved for header data) in the order in which they've appeared each day as recorded by Figure 11-7.

Monday	Tuesday	Wednesday	Thursday	Friday
Danny	Chrissy	Brett	Rosa	Conor
Conor	Brett	Nydia	Chrissy	Robin
Brett	Conor	Conor	Brett	Bennie
Bennie	Rob	Danny	Conor	Nancy
Nydia	Nancy	Bennie	Rob	Nydia
Rosa	Robin	Nancy	Nydia	Danny
Robin	Danny		Bennie	Rob
Rob	Rosa		Danny	
Nancy			Nancy	
Chrissy				

Figure 11-7. *Classifying daily attendance data*

We want to tabulate the attendance totals for each student for the week, and if that plan sounds like another call for COUNTIF you're right. Again, our first order of business is to thresh a unique student listing from the five columns' worth of data. What's different here is the messy reality that the columns are unevenly occupied with names. If we thus write in I4:

$$=SORT(UNIQUE(TOCOL(A2:E11)))$$

The formula will unfurl this roster, per Figure 11-8.

=SORT(UNIQUE(TOCOL(A2:E11)))		
Bennie		
Brett		
Chrissy		
Conor		
Danny		
Nancy		
Nydia		
Rob		
Robin		
Rosa		
0		

Figure 11-8. *Ten students, eleven outcomes*

We see what's happened. Because attendance fell short of 100% on some days, the TOCOL expression picks up on the blanks pock-marking some of the columns and reports them in our single column as a zero, a decision that doesn't serve the outcome very well. But rewriting the formula to read in Figure 11-9

=SORT(UNIQUE(TOCOL(A2:E11,1)))			
Bennie			
Brett			
Chrissy			
Conor			
Danny			
Nancy			
Nydia			
Rob			
Robin			
Rosa			

Figure 11-9. *All present and accounted for – except the blanks*

evicts any blanks from the spill range, a happy consequence of the 1 we've added to the formula (the "ignore blanks" argument), and that looks much better.

And once you've gotten this far you can break out another COUNTIF, dropping it into J4 and brought to our attention by Figure 11-10.

=SORT(UNIQUE(TOCOL(A2:E11,1)))		
Bennie	4	=COUNTIF(A2:E11,I4#)
Brett	4	
Chrissy	3	
Conor	5	
Danny	5	
Nancy	5	
Nydia	4	
Rob	4	
Robin	3	
Rosa	3	

Figure 11-10. *Gold stars for Conor, Danny, and Nancy*

Now what's additionally cool about all this is if I redefine the attendance data as a table (making sure to tick the My table has headers box as you proceed), I can add more names to the attendance data in spite of the jagged table-column heights, and those new entries will be processed by our existing formulas, for example, in Figure 11-11.

Monday	Tuesday	Wednesday	Thursday	Friday
Danny	Chrissy	Brett	Rosa	Conor
Conor	Brett	Nydia	Chrissy	Robin
Brett	Conor	Conor	Brett	Bennie
Bennie	Rob	Danny	Conor	Nancy
Nydia	Nancy	Bennie	Rob	Nydia
Rosa	Robin	Nancy	Nydia	Danny
Robin	Danny		Bennie	Rob
Rob	Rosa		Danny	
Nancy			Nancy	
Chrissy				
Zelda				

=SORT(UNIQUE(TOCOL(A2:E12,1)))		
Bennie	4	=COUNTIF(A2:E12,I4#)
Brett	4	
Chrissy	3	
Conor	5	
Danny	5	
Nancy	5	
Nydia	4	
Rob	4	
Robin	3	
Rosa	3	
Zelda	1	

Figure 11-11. *Zelda is new, reported, and sorted*

147

TOROW Is Slightly Different

And as you've probably inferred, TOROW realigns multi-column data into a single *row's* worth of output, relying on the same arguments as TOCOL but nevertheless sometimes requiring a few more user decisions.

To explain: the above screen shot delineates a sorting of the unique instances of student names with TOCOL; but to sort student names uniquely with TOROW you must write as follows, as we see in Figure 11-12.

=SORT(UNIQUE(TOROW(A2:E11,1),1),,,1)									
Bennie	Brett	Chrissy	Conor	Danny	Nancy	Nydia	Rob	Robin	Rosa

Figure 11-12. *Sideways student sort*

What's different here is that the UNIQUE function must be told to spill the unique names across *columns*, evidenced by the 1 in its final argument (the one preceding the three commas); and SORT too must be asked to order the data horizontally – stipulated by the last 1 in the entire formula.

Note   By default, b*oth* TOCOL and TOROW scan the ranges which they work by *column;* that is, they scan the data horizontally, realigning them into a single column or row one column at a time.

Lining Up the Conclusions

By constricting multi-column data into a single column or row the new TOCOL and TOROW dynamic array functions greatly ease the task of analyzing those data – even if, as we'll see, you want to return them back to multiple columns whence they came. On the other hand, of course, you need to decide if TOCOL and TOROW are in fact the tools you need. For example, you almost surely *won't* want to apply them to multi-field, as opposed to simple multi-column data, for example, these names and test scores in Figure 11-13.

Ted	56
Jane	67
Mary	87

Figure 11-13. *Don't try this at home: jamming two fields into one column*

Put TOCOL to that task and you'll wind up with the following, as in Figure 11-14.

Ted
56
Jane
67
Mary
87

Figure 11-14. *Apples and oranges: Alphas and numerics don't mix*

Try that and you'll be reaching for the undo command pronto.

Coming Attractions

The next chapter will introduce a pair of new functions that can be made to usefully partner with TOCOL and TOROW, WRAPCOLS and WRAPROWS, both of which take the analysis in the opposite direction – by spreading one column's or row's worth of data into multiple columns or rows.

CHAPTER 12

WRAPCOLS and WRAPROWS: Giving Some Direction to the Data

Spreadsheet lists can get long. Remember that an Excel worksheet places over one million rows of potential records at your disposal; and while your data-management needs will likely never push that envelope, your pint-sized laptop screen may not be able to portray the list in its entirety – even if it only runs to 50 records. And if you run out of onscreen room for the list but want to see as much of it as possible you may want, for presentational purposes, to redistribute the data into columns, in the plural. You can't see 300 rows of data at one time, but if you repackage all of them into 15 columns of 20 records each, you probably could.

And that's a job for the new WRAPCOLS and WRAPROWS dynamic array functions, which get a single column's or row's worth of data in their sights and reassign them across a desired number of columns or rows. These are tools for data reorganization, not manipulation, and play a role comparable to the visual enhancing afforded by a pivot table's Slicer. There, if a field contains numerous items, not all of which are visually accessible owing to space limitations, the Slicer can redistribute the items into rows and columns, as seen in Figure 12-1.

A. I. Katz, *Up Up and Array!*, https://doi.org/10.1007/978-1-4842-8966-2_12

Last Name					
Abraham	Adams	Aderholt	Aguilar	Allen	^
Allred	Amash	Amodei	Armstrong	Arrington	
Axne	Babin	Bacon	Baird	Balderson	
Banks	Barr	BarragÃin	Bass	Beatty	
Bera	Bergman	Beutler	Biggs	Bilirakis	
Bishop	Blumen...	Bonamici	Bost	Boyle	
Brady	Brindisi	Brooks	Brown	Brownley	
Buchanan	Buck	Bucshon	Budd	Burchett	v

Figure 12-1. *That's a wrap, Slicer style*

WRAPCOLS and WRAPROWS do something similar, acting as reciprocal functions of sorts for TOCOL and TOROW, which take columns and rows and stuff them into a single column and row. And as we'll see, the two sets of functions can work together, too.

How They're Written

WRAPCOLS and WRAPROWS comprise the same three arguments, though they come at their data at right angles, so to speak. WRAPCOLS looks like this:

$$=WRAPCOLS(vector[range],wrap\_count,pad\_with)$$

I'm not sure why WRAPCOLS – or Microsoft – suddenly chose to label the range of data with WRAPCOLS works a vector, but it did and you needn't worry about it. What's called the wrap count is slightly more thought-provoking, however. In the case of WRAPCOLS that argument – which calls for a value – does *not* ask the user to specify the number of columns into he/she wishes to pour the data. Rather, wrap count identifies the *number of rows* of data each column is to contain.

(And that means in turn that the wrap count argument in WRAPROWS wants to know the number of *columns* you're earmarking for each row.)

Thus if we return to this familiar collection of data in excerpt (file: *WRAPCOLS – list*, with the range name Student), per Figure 12-2

Student
Abby
Abigail
Adam
Adrian
Adriano
Al
Alan
Albio
Alcee
Alexander
Alexandria
Alma
Ami
Andy
Angie
Ann
Anna
Anthony

Figure 12-2. *A single file of data*

and we want to subject the data's 100 records to a column makeover, this formula

=WRAPCOLS(Student,20)

will stock each of its columns with 20 records, as laid out in Figure 12-3.

=WRAPCOLS(Student,20)

Abby	Austin	Bryan	Danny	Dwight
Abigail	Ayanna	Carol	Darin	Earl
Adam	Barbara	Carolyn	Darren	Ed
Adrian	Barry	Cathy	David	Eddie
Adriano	Ben	Cedric	Dean	Elaine
Al	Bennie	Charles	Debbie	Eleanor
Alan	Betty	Charlie	Debra	Elijah
Albio	Bill	Chellie	Denny	Eliot
Alcee	Billy	Cheri	Denver	Elise
Alexander	Blaine	Chip	Derek	Elissa
Alexandria	Bob	Chris	Devin	Emanuel
Alma	Bobby	Chrissy	Diana	Eric
Ami	Bonnie	Christopher	Dina	Filemon
Andy	Brad	Clay	Don	Francis
Angie	Bradley	Colin	Donald	Frank
Ann	Brenda	Collin	Donna	Fred
Anna	Brendan	Conor	Doris	Frederica
Anthony	Brett	Cynthia	Doug	Garret
Antonio	Brian	Dan	Duncan	Gary
Aumua	Bruce	Daniel	Dusty	George

Figure 12-3. *20 x 5*

Put differently, WRAPCOLS does *not* ask the user to enter the desired number of columns, as counter-intuitive as that sounds. Here the five-column result springs indirectly from the instruction to fill each column with 20 records.

And if you were to write the same expression with WRAPROWS instead, the results would display rows of 20 columns each.

Moreover, note that this columnar arrangement installs the names *down* a particular column, before advancing to the next. The names plunging down the first column assume the order in which they appear in the source data. When that column runs out of room, so to speak, the data continue in column two.

Now on to the optional "pad with" argument, one that we first saw in the TEXTSPLIT function and that may well be of particular use here. If, for example, you write

=WRAPCOLS(Student,17)

each resulting column will comprise 17 names; but because the Student range consists of 100 entries, the final column – the sixth, in this case (100/17 will yield a remainder of 15 records in a 17-row column) – will generate this output, for starters, in Figure 12-4.

=WRAPCOLS(Student,17)					
Abby	Anthony	Bradley	Chrissy	Denver	Eleanor
Abigail	Antonio	Brenda	Christoph	Derek	Elijah
Adam	Aumua	Brendan	Clay	Devin	Eliot
Adrian	Austin	Brett	Colin	Diana	Elise
Adriano	Ayanna	Brian	Collin	Dina	Elissa
Al	Barbara	Bruce	Conor	Don	Emanuel
Alan	Barry	Bryan	Cynthia	Donald	Eric
Albio	Ben	Carol	Dan	Donna	Filemon
Alcee	Bennie	Carolyn	Daniel	Doris	Francis
Alexander	Betty	Cathy	Danny	Doug	Frank
Alexandria	Bill	Cedric	Darin	Duncan	Fred
Alma	Billy	Charles	Darren	Dusty	Frederica
Ami	Blaine	Charlie	David	Dwight	Garret
Andy	Bob	Chellie	Dean	Earl	Gary
Angie	Bobby	Cheri	Debbie	Ed	George
Ann	Bonnie	Chip	Debra	Eddie	#N/A
Anna	Brad	Chris	Denny	Elaine	#N/A

Figure 12-4. *Data shortfall: not enough records for each column*

And if you want to eradicate those #N/A messages, you can amend the formula to read, for example,

=WRAPCOLS(Student,17,"")

Or of course you can fill the "pad with" argument with any other text message you wish, for example, "No Record."

And what this means is that a teacher who needs to devise a rapid-fire seating plan for an exam can do so in a matter of seconds. Say her class of 37 students is scheduled to tackle a test in a room that comprises eight rows and five columns. If the names have been written to First Name and Last Name fields in the A and B columns, she could concatenate them via a formula in the C column, for example, by invoking good old pairwise lifting in Figure 12-5.

=A1:A37&" "&B1:B37

Nathalie	Aaberg	Nathalie Aaberg
Hai	Daquino	Hai Daquino
Joslyn	Mccance	Joslyn Mccance
August	Moatz	August Moatz
Letty	Abbamont(	Letty Abbamonte
Raye	Corradino	Raye Corradino
Princess	Lenertz	Princess Lenertz
Ethel	Haroutunia	Ethel Haroutunian
Raven	Hemken	Raven Hemken
Modesta	Bruna	Modesta Bruna
Rosann	Oliven	Rosann Oliven
Eilene	Musni	Eilene Musni
Cesar	Castano	Cesar Castano
Melodi	Havermale	Melodi Havermale
Sherman	Arduini	Sherman Arduini
Kaye	Loyborg	Kaye Loyborg
Shannan	Fairchild	Shannan Fairchild
Deloise	Naughton	Deloise Naughton
Abel	Librizzi	Abel Librizzi
Sona	Haberer	Sona Haberer

Figure 12-5. *Knowing their place; students awaiting seat assignment (from File: WRAPCOLS - demo seating plan)*

And once the names have been so combined and re-established into a single column, she could write

=WRAPCOLS(C1#,8,"")

And each student will have been assigned a seat – in a room with eight rows and five columns visualized in Figure 12-6.

Nathalie Aaberg	Raven Hemken	Shannan Fairchild	Emilio Arkema	Alycia Buford
Hai Daquino	Modesta Bruna	Deloise Naughton	Cecila Leverton	Judi Cheairs
Joslyn Mccance	Rosann Oliven	Abel Librizzi	Shemeka Kitten	Jamey Colosi
August Moatz	Eilene Musni	Sona Haberer	Noel Jelle	Felicita Coluccio
Letty Abbamonte	Cesar Castano	Dane Petteway	Lan Pohlson	Wai Baracani
Raye Corradino	Melodi Havermale	Kyra Pehl	Lea Grandon	
Princess Lenertz	Sherman Arduini	Ginger Muckley	Mariel Oden	
Ethel Haroutunian	Kaye Loyborg	Robbi Clunie	Earl Forlivio	

Figure 12-6. *You may open the question booklet now*

Some Formulaic Teamwork: TOCOL and WRAPCOLS

Now to understand how TOCOL and WRAPCOLS can interact productively, let's return to that number matrix that figured in a TOCOL exercise (file: WRAPCOLS – sort values) reprised in Figure 12-7.

1	3	9	7
2	5	6	3
3	4	8	7
9	2	3	4
5	3	3	8
10	4	7	3
3	6	1	2
4	9	2	9
5	1	7	2
4	2	9	3
5	1	5	9
9	10	1	4

Figure 12-7. *The Matrix, take 2*

Suppose now we want to sort the above values, and then *return* them to their 12 x 4 columnar arrangement – in their sorted state.

First, let's once again reconfigure the data via TOCOL, written to N5 in Figure 12-8.

=TOCOL(G6:J17)
1
3
9
7
2
5
6
3
3
4
8
7
9
2

Figure 12-8. *A column, in the singular*

Then superimpose a SORT upon the expression

$$=SORT(TOCOL(G6:J17))$$

and then layer WRAPCOLS atop it all

$$=WRAPCOLS(SORT(TOCOL(G6:J17)),12)$$

You should see the following, per Figure 12-9.

=WRAPCOLS(SORT(TOCOL(G6:J17)),12)

1	3	4	7
1	3	4	8
1	3	5	8
1	3	5	9
1	3	5	9
2	3	5	9
2	3	5	9
2	3	6	9
2	4	6	9
2	4	7	9
2	4	7	10
3	4	7	10

Figure 12-9. *Multi-functional: multi-column sort result with one formula*

We see that by coordinating the WRAPCOLS, SORT, and TOCOL functions, we're able to sort the values as well as restore the original, presort columnar arrangement.

Resorting to a Re-sort

You'll notice again that the sort proceeds downward. If I wanted the sort to veer horizontally, such that the values streamed across the columns, I could write the following, as we see in Figure 12-10.

=WRAPROWS(SORT(TOCOL(G6:J17)),4)			
1	1	1	1
1	2	2	2
2	2	2	3
3	3	3	3
3	3	3	3
4	4	4	4
4	4	5	5
5	5	5	6
6	7	7	7
7	8	8	9
9	9	9	9
9	9	10	10

Figure 12-10. *Pointing in the right direction: the sort proceeds horizontally*

This one might require a second look. Here we've resorted to WRAPROWS, with the 4 denoting the number of values set to populate each row. The SORT(TOCOL(G6:J17)) segment is identical in both formulas, but this time WRAPROWS takes the sorted results and points them rightward, instead of downward (keep in mind there may be alternative approaches to this formula).

Multi-tasking: A Two-Column Sort by Last Names

Now in light of all of the above, we can recall the last-name sort we conducted in Chapter 10, the one driven by the TEXTAFTER function, and recalled here in Figure 12-11.

Angelina Jolie	Sandra Bullock	=SORTBY(A1:A10,TEXTAFTER(A1:A10," ",-1))			
Emily Dickinson	George Clooney				
George Clooney	Emily Dickinson				
John Paul Sartre	Mick Jagger				
LeBron James	LeBron James				
Meryl Streep	Angelina Jolie				
Michael Jordan	Ricky Lee Jones				
Mick Jagger	Michael Jordan				
Ricky Lee Jones	John Paul Sartre				
Sandra Bullock	Meryl Streep				

Figure 12-11. *Last-name sort redux*

Now perhaps you can guess where this is going. Once the last-name sort is put in place we can impart an additional, attractive touch to the presentation – say, by apportioning the sorted results to two columns, as in Figure 12-12.

Sandra Bullock	Angelina Jolie	=WRAPCOLS(SORTBY(A1:A10,TEXTAFTER(A1:A10," ",-1)),5)			
George Clooney	Ricky Lee Jones				
Emily Dickinson	Michael Jordan				
Mick Jagger	John Paul Sartre				
LeBron James	Meryl Streep				

Figure 12-12. *Sort of cool: a last name sort, spread across two columns*

That's the kind of reordering of names you see in school programs on graduation days.

Coming Up Next

While WRAPCOLS and WRAPROWS offer new and improved viewing opportunities for data, the next pair of functions – VSTACK and HSTACK – makes important contributions to data *analysis* as well. See you next chapter.

CHAPTER 13

VSTACK and HSTACK: What They're About

The new VSTACK and HSTACK dynamic array functions perform a kind of act of rescue for the user; they enormously simplify a time-worn data-management task that much of the time could in fact be largely avoided to begin with.

That task is the business of merging or consolidating data that's been gathered into multiple datasets. A standard example: a freelancer records his income in a series of datasets, each one archiving one year's worth of activity. In this stereotypical but utterly plausible scenario, our gig economist entrusts each year's dataset to a new worksheet tab, begging the obvious analytical question: what does he do if he wants to bring all the data together, say for the purposes of tabulating aggregate earnings by client? Or alternatively, had he allocated a distinct dataset to each client, he'd be similarly challenged to compute earnings by year, or month, etc.

Those kinds of questions have often been put to Excel's primal Consolidate feature, a click-intensive means for referring multiple datasets to this dialog box and realizing aggregate outcomes, as in Figure 13-1.

© Abbott Ira Katz 2023
A. I. Katz, *Up Up and Array!*, https://doi.org/10.1007/978-1-4842-8966-2_13

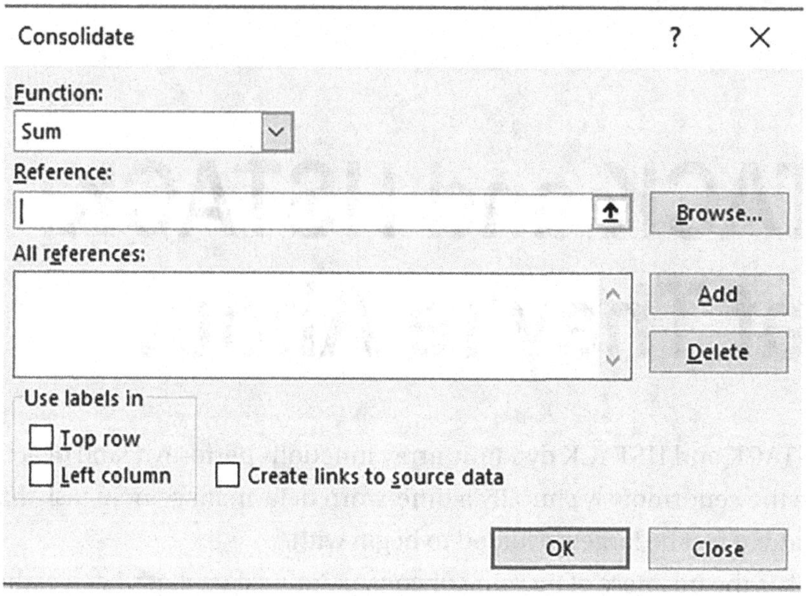

Figure 13-1. *Consolidate – old-school options for merging datasets*

I've never been partial to Consolidate and its ungainly interface, but the larger design question is why a user would nowadays want to frame multiple datasets to begin with. By committing all the data to a *solitary* dataset instead and submitting them all to a pivot table, all sorts of aggregates and field breakouts become possible, and with a notable decrement in effort. Pivot tables are happy to enable year-by-year or client-by-client isolations of the data, and by doing so they stand the consolidation model on its head. After all – it's easier to summon all the data in one place and break out the numbers from there, rather than strew the data across numerous datasets and *then* attempt to reassemble the numbers meaningfully, in Humpty-Dumpty style.

But that's one person's humble and assuredly unasked-for opinion, and my counsel notwithstanding, large numbers of users doubtless continue to practice the multi-dataset policy. And VSTACK and HSTACK have you in mind.

In effect, VSTACK and HSTACK are the new Consolidate. It allows the user, via a very simple formulaic solution, to leave multiple datasets in place while at the same time granting her license to perform a medley of analyses upon them. VSTACK and HSTACK let you have it both ways.

How VSTACK Is Written

VSTACK's syntax is about as easy as it gets:

=VSTACK(range1, range2...)

Again, Excel substitutes "array" for "range," but either term conveys the idea. All you need to do is supply the coordinates of the ranges you wish to stack and VSTACK does the rest. But ease of execution notwithstanding, we'll see that you do need to bring a strategy to your deployment of VSTACK and decide exactly what you want the function to do.

Consider this simple starter example (file: *VSTACK*) of two diminutive datasets that have been posted to the same sheet in D8:F11 and J4:L8 for the ease of visual reference in Figure 13-2.

Name	Id	Score
Jack	36	78
Jill	87	91
Amy	13	66
Janet	45	81

Name	ID	Score
Ted	34	56
Jane	56	89
Mary	12	45

Figure 13-2. Two mini datasets in pre-stack mode

Here we could write

=VSTACK(D8:F11,J4:L8)

And we see the following, per Figure 13-3.

=VSTACK(D8:F11,J4:L8)

Name	ID	Score
Ted	34	56
Jane	56	89
Mary	12	45
Name	Id	Score
Jack	36	78
Jill	87	91
Amy	13	66
Janet	45	81

Figure 13-3. *The headers are stacked against us*

That worked, kind of, but something tells me you won't be completely happy with what you see.

But the fact is that VSTACK has done exactly what we've told it to do. It's stacked both of the ranges we've named, but since the ranges happen to contain the same header row – well, so be it.

Thus we see that VSTACK isn't "smart" – it won't recognize a header row as such and grant it any special status; rather the function will simply deem every row of data as a row of the same species. And so, if you want these stacked ranges to sport but one header, you need to rewrite the formula to

=VSTACK(D8:F11,J5:L8)

Since VSTACK piles the ranges in the order in which they appear in the formula, and since a second header row had been posted to J4, that row needs to be written out, as we've done in Figure 13-4.

=VSTACK(D8:F11,J5:L8)

Name	ID	Score
Ted	34	56
Jane	56	89
Mary	12	45
Jack	36	78
Jill	87	91
Amy	13	66
Janet	45	81

Figure 13-4. *One row purged, two ranges merged*

Another interesting way to stack the ranges while retaining just one header row would be to write the following, as in Figure 13-5.

=UNIQUE(VSTACK(D8:F11,J4:L8))		
Name	ID	Score
Ted	34	56
Jane	56	89
Mary	12	45
Jack	36	78
Jill	87	91
Amy	13	66
Janet	45	81

Figure 13-5. *Avoiding duplication: another way to oust one header row*

Here, because UNIQUE acts upon records exhibiting three cells each, it eliminates one of the identical headers. (Note that while the UNIQUE remedy works for the above scenario, if some of the *records* are fully duplicated, all but one of them will be eliminated by UNIQUE as well. Thus, yet another alternative could be brought to bear on the problem: =VSTACK(D8:F11,DROP(J4:L8,1)). The DROP function parses a specified number of rows from a dataset – in the case of J4:J8, row 1 featuring its header – and will be discussed in Chapter 15.)

But even if you banish one of the headers, VSTACK will continue to regard the remaining one as just another row. If you write the following, per Figure 13-6,

=SORT(VSTACK(D8:F11,J5:L8))		
Amy	13	66
Jack	36	78
Jane	56	89
Janet	45	81
Jill	87	91
Mary	12	45
Name	ID	Score
Ted	34	56

Figure 13-6. *Don't lose your header*

the "header" simply will surrender itself to the sort, unlike bona fide dataset headers that will be left in place.

And what this means, at least in part, is that if you want to treat your newly stacked data as a conventional dataset, you could simply run a Copy > Paste Values over the results, and you're ready to go. Then your headers will remain in place.

But what if you want to VSTACK the ranges while at the same time reserving the right to add *new* records to any of the contributing ranges – and seeing to it that VSTACK will incorporate those new records on the fly?

Not a problem. Just turn each range into a table, as you see in Figure 13-7.

Name ▼	Id ▼	Score ▼
Jack	36	78
Jill	87	91
Amy	13	66
Janet	45	81

Name ▼	ID ▼	Score ▼
Ted	34	56
Jane	56	89
Mary	12	45

Figure 13-7. *Turning the tables on the ranges*

And once that deed is done, write

=VSTACK(Table1, Table2)

And you'll see the following, as in Figure 13-8.

Name	Id	Score
Jack	36	78
Jill	87	91
Amy	13	66
Janet	45	81

Name	ID	Score
Ted	34	56
Jane	56	89
Mary	12	45

=VSTACK(Table1,Table2)

Ted	34	56
Jane	56	89
Mary	12	45
Jack	36	78
Jill	87	91
Amy	13	66
Janet	45	81

Figure 13-8. *VSTACK going live – any new records entered in either table will appear in the stacked result*

The VSTACK formula now references two tables; and because it does, additional data entry to either table will immediately be reflected in the VSTACK output.

Note, by the way, that if I introduce a new record to Table1 – the one whose first entry features the name Ted – that record will insert itself between the name Mary – the last entry in Table1 – and the name Jack, the first record of Table2, illustrated in Figure 13-9.

Name ▼	Id ▼	Score ▼
Jack	36	78
Jill	87	91
Amy	13	66
Janet	45	81

Name ▼	ID ▼	Score ▼
Ted	34	56
Jane	56	89
Mary	12	45
Dan	17	82

=VSTACK(Table1,Table2)		
Ted	34	56
Jane	56	89
Mary	12	45
Dan	17	82
Jack	36	78
Jill	87	91
Amy	13	66
Janet	45	81

Figure 13-9. *Middle of the pack: the new record Dan from Table1 remains among the Table1 data*

That is, Dan won't seek the next available row in the stack; instead, it continues to cast its lot with the other data of Table1. On the other hand, of course, the new records could be sorted, thus overriding their initial positions, per Figure 13-10.

=SORT(VSTACK(Table1,Table2))		
Amy	13	66
Dan	17	82
Jack	36	78
Jane	56	89
Janet	45	81
Jill	87	91
Mary	12	45
Ted	34	56

Figure 13-10. *All together now – data from both tables are sorted together*

When the Data Aren't There

And you've probably noted that when tables are melded by VSTACK, their header rows simply disappear, much as headers vanish from FILTER results. Moreover, if one of the tables featuring in a VSTACK numbers more columns/fields than the others, that discrepancy is inflicted upon the result, as noted by Figure 13-11.

Name	Id	Score	
Jack	36	78	
Jill	87	91	
Amy	13	66	
Janet	45	81	

Name	ID	Score	Subject
Ted	34	56	English
Jane	56	89	Math
Mary	12	45	Soc
Dan	17	82	Poli Sci

=VSTACK(Table1,Table2)

Ted	34	56	English
Jane	56	89	Math
Mary	12	45	Soc
Dan	17	82	Poli Sci
Jack	36	78	#N/A
Jill	87	91	#N/A
Amy	13	66	#N/A
Janet	45	81	#N/A

Figure 13-11. *More than you bargained for; an extra field in one table carries over into VSTACK's results*

We'll learn one simple workaround for this dilemma in the next chapter on the new CHOOSECOLS and CHOOSEROWS functions, and an additional related discussion appears in the chapter on the EXPAND function.

Another Problem, and a Workaround

And there's another subtle VSTACK complication that could pay an unwanted visit to your formula. If any data in the contributing tables happen to be missing – a state of affairs known to befall real-world spreadsheets – those vacant cells show up in a VSTACK as zeros, as in Figure 13-12.

Name	Id	Score
Jack	36	78
Jill	87	
Amy	13	66
Janet	45	81

Name	ID	Score
Ted	34	56
Jane	56	89
Mary		45
Dan	17	82

=VSTACK(Table1,Table2)

Jack	36	78
Jill	87	0
Amy	13	66
Janet	45	81
Ted	34	56
Jane	56	89
Mary	0	45
Dan	17	82

Figure 13-12. *Zeroing in on blank data*

But a blank cell isn't quite a zero. VSTACK misleadingly records Jill's missing test score as 0, when in fact she may have simply missed the exam, and Mary's 0 ID likewise doesn't sound like a number she'd actually be assigned. And moreover, Jill's errant 0 artificially drags the class average down.

Note You can in fact conceal any zeros scattered across a worksheet by clicking File ➤ Options ➤ Advanced ➤ Display Options for this Worksheet and ticking off Show a zero in cells that have zero value. But that decision merely *obscures* the zero from view, and won't suppress its mathematical value. The cell will continue to evaluate to zero.

But help is available. Those pesky zeros can be shown the door with this update to the formula:

=IF(ISBLANK(VSTACK(Table1,Table2)),"",VSTACK(Table1, Table2))

The formula searches the data in both tables for truly blank cells – which again Excel evaluates as zeroes. If it finds any such cells, it performs a kind of redundant substitution; it replaces the blanks with "" – the character expression for a blank, which *won't* be treated as zero. As a result, the formula yields the following in Figure 13-13.

=IF(VSTACK(Table1,Table2)=0,"",VSTACK(Table1,Table2))		
Jack	36	78
Jill	87	
Amy	13	66
Janet	45	81
Ted	34	56
Jane	56	89
Mary		45
Dan	17	82

Figure 13-13. *Let's schedule a makeup exam for Jill*

HSTACK: Not Just VSTACK at a Right Angle

Because datasets treat new *fields* in columns differently from new *records* in rows, the HSTACK function performs a different set of labors in the data-stacking process, even though it's written similarly:

=HSTACK(Range1, Range2...)

HSTACK aligns ranges *alongside* one another, and not atop them, unlike VSTACK. And as a result, HSTACK can perform a very useful data-organization service by extracting selected fields from a larger dataset, thus discarding fields that you decide are irrelevant.

Here's what that means: If we return to that familiar collection of sales data (file: *HSTACK*), with each field again named after its header brought back to in Figure 13-14,

Country	Salesperson	Order Date	OrderID	Order Amount
France	Buchanan	5/27/2019	10249	£ 2,365.76
Mexico	Peacock	5/27/2019	10250	£ 3,597.90
UK	Peacock	5/29/2019	10251	£ 1,552.60
UK	Dodsworth	5/31/2019	10252	£ 896.35
France	Leverling	6/1/2019	10253	£ 654.06
Mexico	Peacock	6/2/2019	10254	£ 1,444.80
UK	King	6/3/2019	10255	£ 517.80
France	Peacock	6/8/2019	10256	£ 1,119.90
Canada	Davolio	6/9/2019	10257	£ 1,142.03
UK	Callahan	6/11/2019	10258	£ 584.00
Mexico	Leverling	6/11/2019	10259	£ 100.80
France	Peacock	6/15/2019	10260	£ 1,504.65
UK	Peacock	6/16/2019	10261	£ 448.00
UK	Dodsworth	8/7/2019	10262	£ 1,873.80
Canada	Leverling	6/17/2019	10263	£ 346.56

Figure 13-14. *More of the same: sales data ripe for HSTACKing*

perhaps we're only interested in the data gleaned from the Country, Salesperson, and Order_Amount fields. If so, we could write

=HSTACK(Country,Salesperson,Order_Amount)

And that expression would yield the following, in excerpt, per Figure 13-15.

=HSTACK(Country,Salesperson,Order_Amount)		
France	Buchanan	2365.76
Mexico	Peacock	3597.90
UK	Peacock	1552.60
UK	Dodsworth	896.35
France	Leverling	654.06
Mexico	Peacock	1444.80
UK	King	517.80
France	Peacock	1119.90
Canada	Davolio	1142.03
UK	Callahan	584.00
Mexico	Leverling	100.80
France	Peacock	1504.65
UK	Peacock	448.00
UK	Dodsworth	1873.80
Canada	Leverling	346.56

Figure 13-15. *Dataset made to order: three fields selected from the original five*

(Again, you'd need to reformat the Order_Amount data suitably. Also, remember that the original field headers aren't returned atop the results, nor do the original field range names somehow carry over to this new mini-dataset.) If you're happy with the way the data look you could next perform a Copy > Paste Values over the data, add a header field, and proceed to treat the new output as a standard, slimmed-down dataset. In addition, recall as always that the HSTACK output is a dynamic array spill range, and so if you've written HSTACK to say, H6, you'd refer to the data in another formula as H6#.

Thus, we see that a bit of irony is at work here. While the two stack functions are meant to fuse independent ranges together into a larger dataset, they can also *reduce* the bulk of existing datasets by tossing out extraneous fields that you don't need, stacking what remains. This capacity of HSTACK for paring larger datasets down to only the fields with which you want to work is a most worthwhile feature, in view of the fact that some datasets contain dozens of fields, many of which simply won't have any relevance to your work with them.

And there's more. If you redefine the original salesperson dataset as a table and continue to enter new records there, those entries will also automatically appear in the HSTACK-generated results too. Indeed – you can even write an HSTACK formula drawn from the salesperson dataset to a *different workbook*, and changes to the source dataset will still be reflected in the HSTACK results.

And one more formula option: if you want to apply HSTACK to a subset of fields from the same dataset and those fields happen to be adjoining, for example, Country, Salesperson, and Order Date, you can also write

=HSTACK(Country:Order_Date)

Using HSTACK to Rearrange the Whole Dataset

And for a related option, if you wanted to edit the order in which *all* the above fields appear, you could write, for example,

=HSTACK(Salesperson,Country,Order_ID,Order_Date,Order_Amount)

Here HSTACK reassigns the positions of all the dataset fields – but again minus the field headers.

And for another similar but not identical example, if we're working with our earlier test-score dataset (file: *HSTACK – student grades*), each of whose fields carries the name of its header, reviewed by Figure 13-16,

name	soc	phil	poli sci	art	physics	chem
Bill	75	90	89	72	89	79
Dana	55	68	87	47	56	50
Ed	61	38	46	36	88	66
Jack	34	80	81	56	57	64
Jane	66	83	30	72	66	56
Hortense	41	85	53	75	90	45
Paul	71	59	69	61	100	72
Ted	66	66	70	35	76	91
Ulysses	59	52	100	94	38	31
Wanda	84	97	35	52	75	86

Figure 13-16. *Exam review, this time with HSTACK*

we could enter a subject name in say, K4, and write the following, as captured by Figure 13-17.

art	
=HSTACK(name,INDIRECT(K4))	
Bill	72
Dana	47
Ed	36
Jack	56
Jane	72
Hortense	75
Paul	61
Ted	35
Ulysses	94
Wanda	52

Figure 13-17. *One formula yielding two independent fields*

The INDIRECT function appropriates the text entry "art" and retools it into a reference to the *range* of the same name.

HSTACK's advantage here is its facility for returning two (or more) distinct fields with *one* formula, but at the same time allowing each field to occupy its own range of cells. By contrast, a string concatenation formula attempting the same thing would have collapsed the fields into *one* range, for example,

=name&" "&INDIRECT(K4)

And returned the data as *text*, thus mandating a round of hoop-jumping in order to disentangle the names from the scores and install the two sets of data into separate columns.

HSTACK and the One-Formula Name Split

Now if we make our way back to that batch of names with which we earlier put out TEXTBEFORE and TEXTAFTER through their pace (here, the file: *HSTACK – separating names*), we can direct HSTACK to a similar name-splitting task, but this time accomplishing the deed with a single formula. Say we want to engineer a name split such that all middle names join with the first names; if so, we can write in B1

=HSTACK(TEXTBEFORE(A1:A10," ",-1),
TEXTAFTER(A1:A10," ",-1))

The first half of the formula searches for all the names preceding the *last* space in the cell, keyed to the negative number that inaugurates the search in a right-to-left direction; the second segment looks out for all names that *follow* the cell's last space, likewise hinging its search on a negative number. HSTACK then welds both expressions into one larger formula, yielding the following, in Figure 13-18.

Angelina Jolie	Angelina	Jolie	=HSTACK(TEXTBEFORE(A1:A10," ",-1),TEXTAFTER(A1:A10," ",-1))
Emily Dickinson	Emily	Dickinson	
George Clooney	George	Clooney	
John Paul Sartre	John Paul	Sartre	
LeBron James	LeBron	James	
Meryl Streep	Meryl	Streep	
Michael Jordan	Michael	Jordan	
Mick Jagger	Mick	Jagger	
Ricky Lee Jones	Ricky Lee	Jones	
Sandra Bullock	Sandra	Bullock	

Figure 13-18. *Plenty of names, one formula*

Of course, we could perform this same feat with many thousands of names, all submitting to that single formula.

Coming Up

While VSTACK and HSTACK can build larger data wholes by amalgamating discrete ranges, the next chapter describes a related pair of functions that modify the sizes of existing datasets through a kind of data *shrinkage* – CHOOSECOLS and CHOOSEROWS. See you soon.

CHAPTER 14

CHOOSECOLS and CHOOSEROWS: Less Is More

Much of the time a dataset warehouses more information than you currently need. That's why data are so often filtered, after all; and the decision to filter can cut back the data from one of two vantage points: you may need to filter the *fields* you need and shun the others, but at other times you may leave all the fields intact and apply the filter to selected *records*. Whichever route you take, the new CHOOSECOLS and CHOOSEROWS dynamic array functions will help point you in the right direction.

We've just learned about the VSTACK and HSTACK functions, the latter of which can pluck a subset of fields from a wider dataset and reap a new dataset from the harvest. CHOOSECOLS does something comparable, but with a few important differences that you'll want to know about.

How CHOOSECOLS Is Written

Like its VSTACK and HSTACK cousins, CHOOSECOLS is easy to write, consisting of two essential arguments:

=CHOOSECOLS(range/array,column_number1,
column_number2…)

(The multiple column number selections in effect reiterate the same argument as needed.) CHOOSECOLS requires as its point of inception an existing range or array, from which you decide which fields – or columns – interest you. And those columns are referred to in straightforward numeric terms.

© Abbott Ira Katz 2023
A. I. Katz, *Up Up and Array!*, https://doi.org/10.1007/978-1-4842-8966-2_14

For example, if we recycle our salesperson data here (file: *CHOOSECOLS*), we can write in G6

$$=CHOOSECOLS(All,1,3,5)$$

That formula asks CHOOSECOLS to prise columns 1, 3, and 5 from the dataset – that is, the Country, Order_Date, and Order_Amount fields, as evoked by Figure 14-1.

=CHOOSECOLS(all,1,3,5)		
France	43612	2365.76
Mexico	43612	3597.9
UK	43614	1552.6
UK	43616	896.35
France	43617	654.06
Mexico	43618	1444.8
UK	43619	517.8
France	43624	1119.9
Canada	43625	1142.03
UK	43627	584
Mexico	43627	100.8
France	43631	1504.65
UK	43632	448
UK	43684	1873.8

Figure 14-1. *Three out of five ain't bad: CHOOSECOLS selects fields from the salesperson data.*

Again, the now-standard cautions about these spilled results need to be recalled: the output could do with some reformatting, and the source field headers are absent, befitting a spilled-range result. And again, if you reconstitute the original salesperson dataset into a table, any new data entry conducted there will automatically be shipped to the above CHOOSECOLS results; that is, the new data remain connected to the old.

Now in fact we carried out an exercise in the previous chapter that resembles the one above; there, too, we charged HSTACK with the task of separating several fields from the one dataset and repackaging them into a fresh one. But what's different here is that CHOOSECOLS identifies the fields by their *column or field numbers,* while HSTACK requires a field *name* or set of range coordinates. And the reason why CHOOSECOLS can work with numbers – simpler references, after all – is because it works with fields belonging to the *same dataset*. Since CHOOSECOLS' first argument asks for a dataset reference, it naturally knows to which number field(s) the ensuing number arguments refer. HSTACK, on the other hand, can amalgamate disconnected fields from anywhere in the workbook (or even beyond), and so must rely on specific field names or range coordinates.

And as with HSTACK, nothing prevents you from resequencing fields with CHOOSECOLS, for example,

=CHOOSECOLS(All,5,3,1)

And just for the record, CHOOSECOLS also allows you to earmark column numbers via negative references that point right to left. Thus

=CHOOSECOLS(All,-1,-3)

will sift and return Order_Amount and Order_Date from the dataset, and in that order. This option might conceivably be of use should you need to reference a field near the far end of a very extensive dataset comprising hundreds of fields. Thus, for example,

=CHOOSECOLS(All,-2)

would extract the next-to-last field of a 279-field dataset, sparing you the chore of knowing to precisely request field number 278.

Keep in mind, however, that this kind of functionality can't be likened to the significance of negative references in the TEXTBEFORE and TEXTAFTER functions; there, negative values identify different positions of the *same delimiter* in a cell in which it appears multiple times (e.g., spaces separating each word), and as such can return *different numbers of words*. Here, the negative numbers always tap a *single* field, as do the positive values.

Teaming with Other Functions

In any event, once you acquaint yourself with the field/column number rule (analogous to the sort index argument in the SORT function, which also requests the *number* of a column/field) you can combine CHOOSECOLS with other useful functions – but you have to proceed with care. This formula

=SORT(CHOOSECOLS(All,1,3,5),2)

will in fact sort the three selected fields by the *second field* cited in the formula, that is, Order_Date. The 2 does *not* refer to Salesperson, which is positioned as the second field in the entire dataset. And so

$$=SORT(CHOOSECOLS(All,1,5,3),2)$$

will deliver a sort driven by the Order_Amount field, which is positioned in second place in the above formula. And this expression

$$=SORT(CHOOSECOLS(All,1,3,5),4)$$

will yield an error message – because CHOOSECOLS has identified only three columns.

On the other hand, CHOOSECOLS will work deftly with the FILTER function, and with great flexibility. To demonstrate, write the salesperson name Peacock in I2 and write in I4

$$=FILTER(CHOOSECOLS(All,1,3,5),Salesperson=I2)$$

You should see the following (in excerpt) via Figure 14-2.

Peacock		
=FILTER(CHOOSECOLS(all,1,3,5),Salesperson=I2)		
Mexico	43612.00	3597.9
UK	43614.00	1552.6
Mexico	43618.00	1444.8
France	43624.00	1119.9
France	43631.00	1504.65
UK	43632.00	448
Mexico	43639.00	3536.6
UK	43654.00	86.5
France	43654.00	155.4
Mexico	43660.00	1170.37
UK	43667.00	80.1
UK	43669.00	1887.6
Canada	43673.00	591.6
Canada	43677.00	349.5
UK	43697.00	516.8

Figure 14-2. Have it your way; choose your columns and your salesperson

The usual formatting issues aside, we see a curious mix and match at work: CHOOSECOLS employs its standard column-number references, while as the FILTER segment insists that we enter a field name – Salesperson – by which the output is filtered. Of course, we're viewing a double filter, as it were – a filter of Peacock's sales activity, filtered in turn by only three of the dataset's fields. And of course, we're filtering for salesperson, even though that field is nowhere to be found in the CHOOSECOLS segment of the formula.

And what this also means is that if we want to filter the data by say, Country – one of the fields that *have* been designated by CHOOSECOLS – we still need to write the formula this way, as in Figure 14-3.

France		
=FILTER(CHOOSECOLS(all,1,3,5),Country=I2)		
France	43612.00	2365.76
France	43617.00	654.06
France	43624.00	1119.9
France	43631.00	1504.65
France	43635.00	1101.2
France	43642.00	642.2
France	43654.00	155.4
France	43670.00	60
France	43671.00	210
France	43675.00	2645
France	43689.00	424
France	43698.00	182.4
France	43704.00	288
France	43708.00	164.4
France	43708.00	982

Figure 14-3. *Vive la formula; filtering for France*

CHOOSECOLS and Too Much Information

In the course of our review of VSTACK in the previous chapter, we encountered a pair of tables, one of which featured an extra field that was treated by VSTACK as follows, reprised in Figure 14-4.

Name	ID	Score	Subject
Ted	34	56	English
Jane	56	89	Math
Mary	12	45	Soc
Dan	17	82	Poli Sci

Name	Id	Score
Jack	36	78
Jill	87	91
Amy	13	66
Janet	45	81

=VSTACK(Table1,Table2)

Ted	34	56	English
Jane	56	89	Math
Mary	12	45	Soc
Dan	17	82	Poli Sci
Jack	36	78	#N/A
Jill	87	91	#N/A
Amy	13	66	#N/A
Janet	45	81	#N/A

Figure 14-4. *One field too many*

We stated then that CHOOSECOLS can afford a swift way out of this dilemma, by enabling us to rewrite the above formula as

=CHOOSECOLS(VSTACK(Table1,Table2),1,2,3)

By restricting the two stacked tables to their first three fields only, the ones that they share, CHOOSECOLS rids the stack of the superfluous fourth field, per Figure 14-5.

Name	Id	Score
Jack	36	78
Jill	87	91
Amy	13	66
Janet	45	81

Name	ID	Score	Subject
Ted	34	56	English
Jane	56	89	Math
Mary	12	45	Soc
Dan	17	82	Poli Sci

=CHOOSECOLS(VSTACK(Table1,Table2),1,2,3)

Ted	34	56
Jane	56	89
Mary	12	45
Dan	17	82
Jack	36	78
Jill	87	91
Amy	13	66
Janet	45	81

Figure 14-5. *Three-column structure, all lined up*

Now the above strategy works for a VSTACK in which you need to *reduce* the field count of one of the stacked datasets. If you need to head in the other direction – that is, you want to *increase* the field count of one of the datasets in order for it to stack properly with another dataset having *more* fields – that task awaits the discussion of the EXPAND function.

In sum, what CHOOSECOLS brings to the process is a far easier way to tap into only those fields that interest you. As you may recall from our FILTER discussions, a pre-CHOOSECOLS take on the above formula might look like this:

=FILTER(INDEX(All,SEQUENCE(ROWS(All)),{1,3,5}),
Salesperson=I2)

Somehow, I suspect you'll prefer the CHOOSECOLS alternative.

CHOOSEROWS: Record-Braking

As we indicated at the outset of the chapter, the two CHOOSE functions perform filtering operations of sorts: CHOOSECOLS excises *fields* from a dataset while retaining others, and CHOOSEROWS gives selected *records* the boot while holding on to a desired remainder.

CHOOSEROWS indeed filters records, but in a relatively coarse manner, if you need to filter all sales conducted in France, or learn which sales exceeded or equalled $2,000, then you'd turn to the FILTER function. CHOOSEROWS can't apply detailed criteria, unlike FILTER's sweeping capabilities; rather, it simply grabs the rows that you specify, which in turn may serve some broader purpose.

To explain: CHOOSEROWS exhibits the same basic syntax as CHOOSECOLS:

=CHOOSEROWS(range/array,row_number1, row_number2...)

Thus, if you call up the *CHOOSEROWS* practice file and enter

=CHOOSEROWS(All,1,2,3,4,5)

you'll return, in Figure 14-6.

=CHOOSEROWS(all,1,2,3,4,5)				
France	Buchanan	43612	10249	2365.76
Mexico	Peacock	43612	10250	3597.9
UK	Peacock	43614	10251	1552.6
UK	Dodsworth	43616	10252	896.35
France	Leverling	43617	10253	654.06

Figure 14-6. *Take five; CHOOSEROWS calls up the first five rows in the dataset*

(Again, you'll be faced with the usual reformatting necessities.)

CHOOSEROWS grants you enormous discretion over which rows you admit to the formula, and in any sequence. These formulas are perfectly proper:

=CHOOSEROWS(All,22,23,24,25,26)

=CHOOSEROWS(All,17,9,24,31,11)

Now for an obvious follow-on question: suppose I want to choose the first 100 rows from a larger dataset. Must I write

=CHOOSEROWS(All,1,2,3,4,5,6,7,8,...)

That is, do I have to key in every row reference from 1 to 100?

I'm glad you asked. The answer: well, no, you don't. You'll be happy to know you can write

=CHOOSEROWS(All,SEQUENCE(100))

Our old friend SEQUENCE can supply all 100 row values. It's a dynamic array formula, after all – with each of the SEQUENCE-spawned values from 1 to 100 choosing the dataset row bearing that number.

And yes, as with CHOOSECOLS, you can tell CHOOSEROWS to proceed with negative values. This formula

$$=CHOOSEROWS(All,-1)$$

will dredge the very last row in the dataset.

Where the Row Count Starts

Another important point: all the row entries in the above formulas denote a row's *relative position in the dataset*, and not its absolute row address. Thus, the number 1 in this expression

$$=CHOOSEROWS(All,1,2,3,4,5)$$

attests to the first row in the *dataset*, irrespective of where the data actually start in the worksheet. 1 always signifies the row position of a dataset's first record – here, the one immediately beneath the header row.

Unique Records in Non-adjacent Fields: Take 2

You may remember our discussion in the chapter devoted to the UNIQUE function about drawing unique records from the data in two non-adjacent fields, one that was hinged upon a fairly ornate application of the INDEX function. But CHOOSECOLS can essay the same task with a far simpler formula.

If you open the *UNIQUE records in non-adjacent fields with CHOOSECOLS* practice file, you'll reacquaint yourself with these salesperson data, in which the Country and Salesperson fields aren't contiguous (in excerpt, Figure 14-7).

Country	Order Date	Salesperson	OrderID	Order Amount	
France	5/27/2019	Buchanan	10249	£	2,365.76
Mexico	5/27/2019	Peacock	10250	£	3,597.90
UK	5/29/2019	Peacock	10251	£	1,552.60
UK	5/31/2019	Dodsworth	10252	£	896.35
France	6/1/2019	Leverling	10253	£	654.06
Mexico	6/2/2019	Peacock	10254	£	1,444.80
UK	6/3/2019	King	10255	£	517.80
France	6/8/2019	Peacock	10256	£	1,119.90
Canada	6/9/2019	Davolio	10257	£	1,142.03
UK	6/11/2019	Callahan	10258	£	584.00
Mexico	6/11/2019	Leverling	10259	£	100.80
France	6/15/2019	Peacock	10260	£	1,504.65
UK	6/16/2019	Peacock	10261	£	448.00
UK	8/7/2019	Dodsworth	10262	£	1,873.80
Canada	6/17/2019	Leverling	10263	£	346.56

Figure 14-7. *Salespersons in far-off Countries*

If we again want to develop a list of all the unique combinations of countries and salespersons, but propelled this time by CHOOSECOLS, the journey exhibits far fewer bumps, as witnessed in Figure 14-8 (in excerpt).

=UNIQUE(CHOOSECOLS(All,1,3))	
Country	Salesperson
France	Buchanan
Mexico	Peacock
UK	Peacock
UK	Dodsworth
France	Leverling
UK	King
France	Peacock
Canada	Davolio
UK	Callahan
Mexico	Leverling
Canada	Leverling

Figure 14-8. Bye, bye INDEX – CHOOSECOLS for a smoother ride

Here, the formula simply calculates every unique combination of the records drawn from the dataset's first and third column – the ones containing Country and Salesperson. It's so easy you'll think you did something wrong.

Using CHOOSEROWS to Fill in the Blanks

Now you may remember a few of the exercises we described in the FILTER chapter aiming to filter a dataset rife with blank rows. Now let's direct CHOOSEROWS to those data, and demonstrate how the function can easily *eliminate* all those rows and thus craft an eminently usable dataset (file: *CHOOSEROWS – blank rows*).

But first, we need to review the way in which CHOOSEROWS enumerates the rows with which it works. Remember that our dataset, bearing our usual default name of All and featuring 3788 rows, actually commences in row 2 (see the introductory notes in Chapter 3 under the "Field Notes: Field and Dataset Names" heading). And that row – row number 1 *in the dataset*, the one immediately beneath the header row – is *blank*. That means that the first data-bearing row in the dataset is, in the language of CHOOSEROWS, row 2.

Moreover, we know that every other row in the dataset is empty – that is, all the *odd-numbered dataset rows,* inaugurated by dataset row 1. With that information in tow, we can click into Sheet 1 of the practice file and write, in B2

=CHOOSEROWS(All,SEQUENCE(1894,,2,2))

An expression that yields the following (in excerpt) in Figure 14-9.

=CHOOSEROWS(All,,SEQUENCE(1894,,2,2))													
82	Rufus King	148-15	90 AVE	4	New Cons HPD	0	659	1	1	24515	30100			
82	Rufus King	148-15	90 AVE	4	New Cons HPD	0	802	3	1	29418	36120			
82	Rufus King	148-15	90 AVE	4	New Cons HPD	1	709	2	1	26298	30100	2	26298	34400
82	Rufus King	148-15	90 AVE	4	New Cons HPD	1	863	12	1	31578	36120	2	31578	41280
82	Rufus King	148-15	90 AVE	4	New Cons HPD	2	1044	23	2	37852	41280	3	37852	46440	4
82	Rufus King	148-15	90 AVE	4	New Cons HPD	3	1199	5	3	43749	46440	4	43749	51540	5
83	Norman T	90-14	161 STREE	4	New Cons HDC	0	500	1	1	19406	29400			
83	Norman T	90-14	161 STREE	4	New Cons HDC	0	1012	3	1	36960	52920			
83	Norman T	90-14	161 STREE	4	New Cons HDC	0	1250	3	1	45120	94080			
83	Norman T	90-14	161 STREE	4	New Cons HDC	1	516	3	1	20023	23520	2	20023	26880
83	Norman T	90-14	161 STREE	4	New Cons HDC	1	640	11	1	24275	29400	2	24275	33600
83	Norman T	90-14	161 STREE	4	New Cons HDC	1	1294	28	1	46698	52920	2	46698	60480
83	Norman T	90-14	161 STREE	4	New Cons HDC	1	1450	30	1	52046	107520	2	52046	107520
83	Norman T	90-14	161 STREE	4	New Cons HDC	2	774	5	2	28938	33600	3	28938	37800	4

Figure 14-9. *Nothin' but data: blank rows removed*

How does this formula work? Its SEQUENCE element requests 1894 rows – half of the 3798 rows contributing to the dataset, and thus the number of rows containing data. It kicks off its sequence with the number 2 – again, representing the first row in the dataset featuring data – and increments each following value by a step of 2. Thus, CHOOSEROWS is presented with row values 2,4,6,8...3798, each corresponding to a row armed with data – and proceeds to choose precisely, and only, those rows.

If that looks good and you want the results to serve as your dataset for subsequent analysis, you can aim a Copy > Paste Values routine at the spill range – and remember, it *is* a spill range. Next, you can copy and paste the original headers above it all, and you're ready to go – just range-name each field via Create from Selection.

Coming Next: Subjecting Rows and Columns to a Different TAKE

You'll see that the next pair of new dynamic array functions we'll examine bear a family resemblance to CHOOSECOLS and CHOOSEROWS, but they certainly don't qualify as identical twins. They're called TAKE and DROP, and you'll see what they share in common with the two CHOOSE functions – and what they don't.

CHAPTER 15

TAKE and DROP: Selecting and Rejecting the Data

Similar – but Different

As with CHOOSECOLS and CHOOSEROWS, the new dynamic array TAKE and DROP functions trim datasets by temporarily removing unwanted records and keeping others. But TAKE and DROP do the trimming in ways that are less flexible than the options offered by the two CHOOSE functions – but at the same time, we'll see that they can carry out certain tasks more efficiently.

How They're Written

TAKE and DROP literally proceed in different directions, a distinction that needs to be explained, but they're written in similar ways. TAKE looks like this:

=TAKE(range/array,rows,columns)

(The rows and columns arguments are optional, though you need to supply at least one of them.)

Considering rows for starters, TAKE earns its name by returning, or taking, a specified number of rows from the *uppermost rows in the range* by default. Thus if we open the *TAKE and DROP* practice file consisting of the same names with which we worked in the TEXBEFORE/AFTER chapter (I've named the range here names) and write

=TAKE(names,6)

© Abbott Ira Katz 2023
A. I. Katz, *Up Up and Array!*, https://doi.org/10.1007/978-1-4842-8966-2_15

you'll see the following in Figure 15-1.

Angelina Jolie		
Emily Dickinson		
George Clooney		=TAKE(names,6)
John Paul Sartre		Angelina Jolie
LeBron James		Emily Dickinson
Meryl Streep		George Clooney
Michael Jordan		John Paul Sartre
Mick Jagger		LeBron James
Ricky Lee Jones		Meryl Streep
Sandra Bullock		

Figure 15-1. *A little off the top: TAKE returns the first six names in the range*

That's pretty self-evident, and it discloses an essential premise of TAKE's way of working: unlike CHOOSEROWS, the 6 identifies not a row number, *but the number of cells to be taken from the top of the range.* While CHOOSEROWS enables you to write this expression

=CHOOSEROWS(names,3,1,5)

which pulls rows 3, 1, and 5 from the dataset, you can't issue a multi-row set of references with TAKE.

By the same token, the optional columns argument specifies by default the number of columns *to be taken from the left of the dataset.* Thus, by way of quick demo, this formula written to our trusty salesperson dataset:

=TAKE(all,8,3)

would lift the first eight rows of the data, along with their *first three columns*, per Figure 15-2.

=TAKE(all,8,3)		
France	Buchanan	5/27/2019
Mexico	Peacock	5/27/2019
UK	Peacock	5/29/2019
UK	Dodsworth	5/31/2019
France	Leverling	6/1/2019
Mexico	Peacock	6/2/2019
UK	King	6/3/2019
France	Peacock	6/8/2019

Figure 15-2. *Eight down, three across: TAKE's take-up of row and column data*

This formula

$$=TAKE(all,,3)$$

would conscript *all* the rows, and the first three columns.

By default, then, TAKE can only haul off data from *consecutive* rows and/or columns emanating from the top rows of a dataset, and their leftmost columns. You can't deploy TAKE to deliver *non-consecutive* rows or columns, as you can with CHOOSEROWS or CHOOSECOLUMNS; nor can you take data from a starting point midway into the dataset.

But those are the defaults. As with CHOOSEROWS and CHOOSECOLUMNS, TAKE and DROP will accept negative-numbered arguments. If you write

$$=TAKE(names,-3)$$

you'll take the names occupying the *last three* rows of the dataset, as in Figure 15-3.

Angelina Jolie		
Emily Dickinson		
George Clooney	=TAKE(names,-3)	
John Paul Sartre	Mick Jagger	
LeBron James	Ricky Lee Jones	
Meryl Streep	Sandra Bullock	
Michael Jordan		
Mick Jagger		
Ricky Lee Jones		
Sandra Bullock		

Figure 15-3. *Reversing one's field: TAKE calls up the names from the bottom of the range with its negative argument*

By the same token, referencing the column argument with a negative value will initiate a column grab from the rightmost column. But here, too, TAKE gathers data from the extremes – the very bottom of the data moving upwards, and the far-right columns proceeding towards the left.

DROP: Leaving the Data Behind

The DROP function is considerably less "intuitive" than TAKE, because it forces us to think about the data we *don't* want to use. Befitting its name, DROP specifies the rows and columns that it wants to *exclude* from its results, even as its syntax virtually replicates that of TAKE:

$$=DROP(range/array,rows,columns)$$

Again, the rows and columns arguments are optional, though of course you need to select at least one of them.

For example, this formula written to the practice file

$$=DROP(names,3)$$

will *ignore* the names in the first three rows, per Figure 15-4.

Angelina Jolie		
Emily Dickinson		
George Clooney		=DROP(names,3)
John Paul Sartre		John Paul Sartre
LeBron James		LeBron James
Meryl Streep		Meryl Streep
Michael Jordan		Michael Jordan
Mick Jagger		Mick Jagger
Ricky Lee Jones		Ricky Lee Jones
Sandra Bullock		Sandra Bullock

Figure 15-4. *DROP from the top: the first three rows are disinvited*

And this formula, written to the salesperson data

=DROP(all,,4)

will return all their rows but will *drop*, or eliminate, the first four *fields*, returning the data from column 5 *only*. Again, the 4 doesn't refer to column number four, but rather the *number of columns to be ignored* or dropped, starting from the left of the dataset.

Got that? And yes, DROP will implement negative numbers, too, the better to deepen your confusion. This formula

=DROP(names,-4)

will ignore, or drop, the *last* four names in the range. And that means that these formulas yield equivalent results, brought together in Figure 15-5.

Angelina Jolie			
Emily Dickinson			
George Clooney			
John Paul Sartre		=DROP(names,-4)	=TAKE(names,6)
LeBron James		Angelina Jolie	Angelina Jolie
Meryl Streep		Emily Dickinson	Emily Dickinson
Michael Jordan		George Clooney	George Clooney
Mick Jagger		John Paul Sartre	John Paul Sartre
Ricky Lee Jones		LeBron James	LeBron James
Sandra Bullock		Meryl Streep	Meryl Streep

Figure 15-5. *Either way, you end up with the same names: two formulas, one result*

And once you recognize where DROP and TAKE's respective routes take you, two realizations should emerge: (1) many outcomes orchestrated by TAKE can be achieved as well by DROP, once you understand how their arguments get turned inside out, and (2) because TAKE and DROP can only process *contiguous* rows, you'll very often need to sort the dataset before you can proceed – because the records that you'll want to take or drop have to be atop one another, and also must be situated at the very top or the bottom of the range before you.

Some Real-World Uses

One job that TAKE can accomplish most efficiently is a ranking of data, for example, a list of the ten largest sales in a dataset (file: *TAKE – ranking data*). And while as is often the case in Excel, alternative approaches to the problem might be on hand – via say, the FILTER function – the TAKE alternative is notably slimmer. Here's the FILTER rendition of a top-10 calculation:

=SORT(FILTER(All,RANK(Order_Amount,Order_Amount)<=10),5,-1)

Now compare the above to the TAKE version and the comparison in Figure 15-6.

=TAKE(SORT(all,5,-1),10)

=SORT(FILTER(all,RANK(Order_Amount,Order_Amount)<=10),5,-1)						=TAKE(SORT(all,5,-1),10)				
UK	Fuller	12/30/2020	10880	16387.5		UK	Fuller	44195	10880	16387.5
Mexico	Davolio	2/17/2021	10979	15810		Mexico	Davolio	44244	10979	15810
Canada	King	3/14/2021	11042	12615.05		Canada	King	44269	11042	12615.1
Mexico	Dodsworth	1/10/2021	10902	11380		Mexico	Dodsworth	44206	10902	11380
Canada	Peacock	12/15/2019	10432	11188.4		Canada	Peacock	43814	10432	11188.4
UK	Leverling	11/30/2020	10821	10952.84		UK	Leverling	44165	10821	10952.8
UK	Leverling	1/12/2021	10905	10835.24		UK	Leverling	44208	10905	10835.2
Canada	Leverling	2/6/2020	10487	10495.6		Canada	Leverling	43867	10487	10495.6
UK	Leverling	4/30/2020	10572	10191.7		UK	Leverling	43951	10572	10191.7
France	Fuller	9/8/2020	10715	10164.8		France	Fuller	44082	10715	10164.8

Figure 15-6. *TAKE's top ten tops FILTER's top ten*

Here the TAKE formula on the right sorts, via the highest-to-lowest option (the -1 planted inside the SORT formula), the fifth column of the dataset – the one containing the sales order amounts. It next goes on to take the first ten rows of the sorted output, matching FILTER's output with considerably less keystroking. (Note that this top ten is technically problematic; if two equivalent sales figures hold the tenth position, the TAKE formula depicted above will return only one of them.)

Now what if you wanted to confine the top-ten results to say, the salesperson name and order amount? That's an assignment TAKE can't fulfill on its own, because salesperson and order amount are aligned in the second and fifth columns of the dataset – and TAKE can only reap adjoining fields that occupy the left or right edges of the data. As a result, we need to recruit the more agile CHOOSEROWS to help us complete the task, depicted by Figure 15-7.

=TAKE(SORT(CHOOSECOLS(all,2,5),2,-1),10)	
Fuller	16387.50
Davolio	15810.00
King	12615.05
Dodsworth	11380.00
Peacock	11188.40
Leverling	10952.84
Leverling	10835.24
Leverling	10495.60
Leverling	10191.70
Fuller	10164.80

Figure 15-7. *Teamwork: TAKE and CHOOSECOLS deliver top 10 sales by salesperson*

CHOOSECOLS specifies that only the second (Salesperson) and fifth (Order Amount) columns/fields are to be returned.

A Unique Exercise

You can also let TAKE streamline the answer to a spreadsheet challenge that's been described by several spreadsheet experts on the web. The task: to generate a set of ten *unique* random numbers between say 1 and 50. While of course the RANDARRAY function can unleash thousands or even millions of random values upon your worksheet, it *can't* guarantee that none of the values will repeat. But you can write this expression (try this on a blank worksheet):

=TAKE(SORTBY(SEQUENCE(50),RANDARRAY(50)),10)

And achieve something like Figure 15-8.

=TAKE(SORTBY(SEQUENCE(50),RANDARRAY(50)),10)
8
23
34
36
40
9
1
22
30
47

Figure 15-8. *Random – and unique – values, each somewhere between 1 and 50*

This formula sequences a set of values 1 through 50 (of course you can select any span you wish). It sorts these by a virtual, parallel set of 50 random numbers courtesy of RANDARRAY, and when the sort is executed TAKE simply goes ahead and lops off the first ten rows from the 50 results. Because the SEQUENCE function furnishes 50 consecutive values 1 through 50, these must be unique by definition; sorting them randomly then throws those values into some unpredictable order, from which TAKE grabs the first 10.

More Ranking – but by Percentages

In addition to combing the data for an absolute top ten of values, TAKE can drum up results that yield a given *percent* of the records. Remaining with the *TAKE – ranking data* practice file – suppose that we want to serve up the top 15% of sales orders, a requirement that forces us to deal with an immediate, prior question: since the dataset comprises 798 records 15% of which amounts to 119.7, then somewhere in the formula a rounding off of that value has to be effected.

With that little complication in mind let's enter the following in H6:

=TAKE(SORT(all,5,-1),ROWS(all)*0.15)

That expression should yield (in excerpt) what you see in Figure 15-9.

=TAKE(SORT(all,5,-1),ROWS(all)*0.15)

UK	Fuller	44195	10880	16387.5
Mexico	Davolio	44244	10979	15810
Canada	King	44269	11042	12615.1
Mexico	Dodsworth	44206	10902	11380
Canada	Peacock	43814	10432	11188.4
UK	Leverling	44165	10821	10952.8
UK	Leverling	44208	10905	10835.2
Canada	Leverling	43867	10487	10495.6
UK	Leverling	43951	10572	10191.7
France	Fuller	44082	10715	10164.8
Mexico	Fuller	43930	10549	9921.3
France	Buchanan	43764	10379	9210.9
UK	King	43813	10430	9194.56
Canada	Fuller	44265	11035	8902.5
UK	Leverling	43923	10542	8623.45
UK	King	43750	10365	8593.28
UK	Peacock	44187	10865	8446.45

Figure 15-9. *The top 15% of sales, more or less*

If you've been clicking – and counting – along, you've observed that our formula returns 119 records, a round-down of the decimal-punctuated 119.7. As for the formula itself, it sorts the order amounts highest-to-lowest and brings in the ROWS function to supply the rows argument that counts the number of rows in the order_amount field and multiplies that figure by .15. If you want to round 119.7 upwards, you can edit the formula to read

=TAKE(SORT(all,5,-1),ROUNDUP(ROWS(all)*0.15,0))

That tweak will lift 119.7 to the next integer – 120 – and rank that many records.

And for a more responsive, facile formula, you could of course post the desired percent to a cell instead, say H3, and modify the percent entry there as you wish (with or without ROUNDUP):

=TAKE(SORT(all,5,-1),ROWS(all)*H3)

Letting It DROP: Removing Lowest Grades

Suppose you're a teacher who's assigned eight tests to your students across the term. Since you want to do the right thing, you decide to compute each student's average on the basis of their six highest scores, that is, you're prepared to discard the lowest two.

That sounds like a job made for the DROP function, and it's surely up to the task. Open the *DROP – lowest test* score practice file and try this formula in cell J2, for starters:

=DROP(SORT(B2:I2,,,1),,2)

Again, as per the standard DROP/TAKE strategy we're subjecting the scores in the first *row* – the one housing Bill's test scores – to a sort, this time in a columnar orientation as indicated by the 1 inside the SORT parentheses. We're then commanding DROP to oust the scores in the first two *columns* of the spill range, as confirmed by the final 2 in the formula. You should see something like Figure 15-10.

name	1	2	3	4	5	6	7	8							
Bill	87	47	39	64	41	30	86	100	41	47	64	86	87	100	=DROP(SORT(B2:I2,,,1),,2)
Dana	76	39	57	48	92	72	93	99							
Ed	65	95	76	50	100	80	69	88							
Jack	42	68	61	78	90	39	38	56							
Jane	95	74	57	88	76	63	71	32							
Hortense	30	48	68	95	72	52	65	56							
Paul	32	87	43	96	53	72	42	94							
Ted	86	39	30	47	91	35	49	91							
Ulysses	99	38	50	99	92	75	56	50							
Wanda	49	91	67	96	46	48	90	35							
Jack	87	39	47	97	55	70	77	33							

Figure 15-10. *Bill's in luck: his two lowest scores never happened*

Note the DROP formula spills six results across the row, having jettisoned Bill's two-lowest 30 and 39. Now we can wrap the standard AVERAGE function around DROP, culminating in a single-cell result flashed in Figure 15-11 and formatted as you wish:

name	1	2	3	4	5	6	7	8		
Bill	87	47	39	64	41	30	86	100	70.833	=AVERAGE(DROP(SORT(B2:I2,,,1),,2))

Figure 15-11. *Bill's average for all of eight exams: 61.75*

If that all looks good, we can simply copy the revised formula down the range for each student, as in Figure 15-12.

name	1	2	3	4	5	6	7	8		
Bill	87	47	39	64	41	30	86	100	70.833	=AVERAGE(DROP(SORT(B2:I2,,,1),,2))
Dana	76	39	57	48	92	72	93	99	81.5	=AVERAGE(DROP(SORT(B3:I3,,,1),,2))
Ed	65	95	76	50	100	80	69	88	84.667	=AVERAGE(DROP(SORT(B4:I4,,,1),,2))
Jack	42	68	61	78	90	39	38	56	65.833	=AVERAGE(DROP(SORT(B5:I5,,,1),,2))
Jane	95	74	57	88	76	63	71	32	77.833	=AVERAGE(DROP(SORT(B6:I6,,,1),,2))
Hortense	30	48	68	95	72	52	65	56	68	=AVERAGE(DROP(SORT(B7:I7,,,1),,2))
Paul	32	87	43	96	53	72	42	94	74.167	=AVERAGE(DROP(SORT(B8:I8,,,1),,2))
Ted	86	39	30	47	91	35	49	91	67.167	=AVERAGE(DROP(SORT(B9:I9,,,1),,2))
Ulysses	99	38	50	99	92	75	56	50	78.5	=AVERAGE(DROP(SORT(B10:I10,,,1),,2))
Wanda	49	91	67	96	46	48	90	35	73.5	=AVERAGE(DROP(SORT(B11:I11,,,1),,2))
Jack	87	39	47	97	55	70	77	33	72.167	=AVERAGE(DROP(SORT(B12:I12,,,1),,2))

Figure 15-12. *Making the grade(s): six-pack of test scores*

Up Next

The next, and final, second-generation dynamic array function we'll review is one that at first blush seems slightly curious, one that seems to offer a kind of polar opposite to TAKE and DROP. While those functions narrow the data with which the user wants to work, the function that follows – EXPAND – can make room for data that's yet to be entered. I told you it seems curious; so just turn the page.

CHAPTER 16

EXPAND: Bulking Up the Data

If truth be told, my own introduction to the EXPAND function could be termed slightly mystifying. In his preview of Excel's second-generation dynamic array functions, Microsoft developer Joe McDaid tells us that "EXPAND allows you to grow an array to the size of your choice—you just need to provide the new dimensions and a value to fill the extra space with."

Apart from dangling a preposition, that description left me ever-so-slightly clueless. Exactly what does growing an array (or range) mean, and more to the point, what purpose might that capability serve for you and me?

How It's Written – and Why

But before we try our hand at an answer or two, let's see what EXPAND looks like:

=EXPAND(range/array,rows,columns,pad_with)

As usual, the range/array argument calls for the coordinates of the data with which you're working. The optional rows argument asks for the number of rows to which you want to expand the spill range; if omitted, the argument will simply supply the number of rows featuring in the range. The optional columns parameter likewise requests the number of columns across which the EXPAND spill range will extend, and as with other functions we've seen here, "pad with" enables the user to post a message to cells that would, as we'll see, otherwise transmit an error message.

All of which raises an obvious question for the mystified among us: why would you ask EXPAND to output a complement of rows or columns that exceeds the row and/or column totals of the data you already have?

© Abbott Ira Katz 2023
A. I. Katz, *Up Up and Array!*, https://doi.org/10.1007/978-1-4842-8966-2_16

To take some halting steps toward an answer, let's open the *EXPAND* practice file and observe the range in D8:E12 portrayed in Figure 16-1.

Name	ID
Ted	34
Jane	56
Mary	12
Dan	17

Figure 16-1. *Going big: data to be EXPANDed*

With those data in hand, let's write the following EXPAND formula, say in N13:

=EXPAND(D9:E12,,3)

(Note that the range referenced excludes the header row, per our discussion in the chapter on VSTACK and HSTACK. Note in addition the omission of the rows argument, which defaults that result to the number of rows in the source data.)

You should see the following, per Figure 16-2.

=EXPAND(D9:E12,,3)		
Ted	34	#N/A
Jane	56	#N/A
Mary	12	#N/A
Dan	17	#N/A

Figure 16-2. *One new column, four new #N/A messages*

That Question – Again

That result merely confirms our question. We see that the third column EXPAND has instated is vacant, and since spreadsheets abhor a vacuum, its empty cells have been waylaid by those unlovely #N/A messages you'll probably want to lose. If so, you can rewrite EXPAND

=EXPAND(D9:E12,,3,"no data")

And that "pad with" corrective will adjust the outcomes captured in Figure 16-3.

=EXPAND(D9:E12,,3,"no data")		
Ted	34	no data
Jane	56	no data
Mary	12	no data
Dan	17	no data

Figure 16-3. *No data, but no #N/As*

But still, that cosmetic improvement doesn't address the question: why do we need that third column?

Spreadsheet savant Leila Gharani suggests this reply: we need the third column if we want to merge the above results with *another* dataset, for example, the range in J4:L8, via the VSTACK function. Thus, if we write

=VSTACK(J5:L8,EXPAND(D9:E12,,3,"no data"))

we'll see the following, in Figure 16-4.

=VSTACK(J5:L8,EXPAND(D9:E12,,3,"no data"))		
Jack	36	78
Jill	87	81
Amy	13	66
Janet	45	81
Ted	34	no data
Jane	56	no data
Mary	12	no data
Dan	17	no data

Figure 16-4. *A fitting result with VSTACK and EXPAND*

We thus learn that the phantom third column we had tacked onto D9:E12 with EXPAND now places that range into alignment with the similarly three-columned J5:L8; and perhaps more to the point, the "pad with" caption fills the column with useful, presentable information – "no data" – and in fact, that embellishment turns out to be the real justification for using EXPAND at all.

Indeed – if we write

=VSTACK(J5:L8,EXPAND(D9:E12,,3))

in which the EXPAND expression omits any "pad with" message, we'll wind up with the tableau elaborated in Figure 16-5.

=VSTACK(J5:L8,EXPAND(D9:E12,,3))		
Jack	36	78
Jill	87	81
Amy	13	66
Janet	45	81
Ted	34	#N/A
Jane	56	#N/A
Mary	12	#N/A
Dan	17	#N/A

Figure 16-5. *Conspicuous by its absence; no "pad with" message*

And that is *precisely the same outcome* we'll realize even if we disregard EXPAND altogether and write

=VSTACK(J5:L8,D9:E12)

Thus we see that by *not* invoking the "pad with" argument, an error-free stacking of multiple datasets may not be enabled – even if the newfangled EXPAND is brought into the formula.

Now About Those Zeroes...

And since we've wandered into the error-handling department, let's reconsider the unwanted zeroes that infiltrated our look of the VSTACK function, for example, Figure 16-6.

Name	Id	Score
Jack	36	78
Jill	87	
Amy	13	66
Janet	45	81

Name	ID	Score
Ted	34	56
Jane	56	89
Mary		45
Dan	17	82

=VSTACK(Table1,Table2)

Jack	36	78
Jill	87	0
Amy	13	66
Janet	45	81
Ted	34	56
Jane	56	89
Mary	0	45
Dan	17	82

Figure 16-6. *Nothing doing: zeroes replacing blanks in cells in the VSTACK output*

(Note in the VSTACK exercise the datasets were restructured as tables.) There, VSTACK substituted a zero value for any blank cell among the data it was asked to stack, and that fomented a problem. Returning to our EXPAND practice file, we see that EXPAND will do the same; that is, when it encounters a blank cell, EXPAND will likewise replace the blank with a zero, as we see in Figure 16-7.

Name	ID	
Ted	34	
Jane	56	
Mary		
Dan	17	

=EXPAND(D9:E12,,3,"")

Ted	34	
Jane	56	
Mary	0	
Dan	17	

Figure 16-7. *More of the same; EXPAND also returns a zero to a blank cell, but the "" pad-with argument introduces blanks to the third, expanded column only*

Note here that the blank-character indicator "" applied to the "pad with" argument *does* fill the third, expanded column with blanks – but it doesn't eradicate the zero among the actual *source* data for Mary.

But we can ultimately rid ourselves of the zeroes here, too, but with a formula that entails a bit of cheating – because it bypasses the EXPAND function altogether. If our EXPAND file data were to look like this, as in Figure 16-8,

				Name	ID		Score	
				Jack		36		78
				Jill		87		
				Amy		13		66
Name	ID			Janet		45		81
Ted		34						
Jane		56						
Mary								
Dan		17						

Figure 16-8. *Uninhabited addresses – blank cells to be stacked*

and if we want to stack the two datasets, we could write

=IF(isblank(VSTACK(J5:L8,D9:F12)),"",VSTACK(J5:L8,D9:F12))

You'll note of course that EXPAND isn't even there, having been supplanted by a simple range reference: D9:F12 – and that's an odd one to be sure, because the actual data populating the range only appear in columns D and E. The F column seems to be nothing but a sly, fictitious placeholder, and it is – except for the fact that it represents a third column, and so expands (there's that word) that artificial range to enable it to line up with the three-column J5:L8. D through F can now line up with J through L – because each comprises three columns.

The IF statement above recognizes a spreadsheet reality that we described in the VSTACK chapter – that Excel evaluates blank cells mathematically as zeroes. Thus, the formula here states that any cell reckoned as a zero will receive the blank-character "", and all other cells will be stacked per their actual value, embodied in Figure 16-9.

Name	ID	Score
Jack	36	78
Jill	87	
Amy	13	66
Janet	45	81

Name	ID
Ted	34
Jane	56
Mary	
Dan	17

=IF(ISBLANK(VSTACK(J5:L8,D9:F12)),"",VSTACK(J5:L8,D9:F12))

Jack	36	78
Jill	87	
Amy	13	66
Janet	45	81
Ted	34	
Jane	56	
Mary		
Dan	17	

Figure 16-9. *The zeroes have been blanked out*

We've thus managed to stack the columns properly, while at the same time shedding the default zeroes that VSTACK assigns to blank cells.

So Do We Even Need EXPAND?

The exercise above – in which we seem to have beaten back the misleading zeroes that VSTACK imparts to blank cells, *without* the EXPAND function – suggests in turn that perhaps we could do without EXPAND altogether; but that conclusion isn't quite justified.

For one thing, if the data to be stacked are remodelled as *tables,* that means among other things that the VSTACK will be able to absorb and stack new records as they're entered in the contributing tables. And if so, the VSTACK expression *will* need EXPAND.

To demonstrate, if we revamp our exercise datasets into tables but with some missing data, for example, in Figure 16-10,

Name ▾	ID ▾	Score ▾
Jack	36	78
Jill	87	
Amy	13	66
Janet	45	81

Name ▾	ID ▾
Ted	34
Jane	56
Mary	
Dan	17

Figure 16-10. *Tables for two*

we'll discover that this formula

=VSTACK(Table1,EXPAND(Table2,,3,""))

continues to preserve those zeroes, alas, confirmed by Figure 16-11.

=VSTACK(Table1,EXPAND(Table2,,3,""))		
Jack	36	78
Jill	87	0
Amy	13	66
Janet	45	81
Ted	34	
Jane	56	
Mary	0	
Dan	17	

Figure 16-11. *Nothing to add – return of the zeroes*

But a table *can't* accommodate a dummy, placeholder column that can be stacked above or below a column in the other table, unlike our previous exercise and its dummy field. If we want both datasets to be able to contribute new records to a VSTACK, both must be defined as a table – and if one of them has fewer columns than the other, EXPAND must enter the formula and add that new column, as duly noted in Figure 16-12.

=IF(ISBLANK(VSTACK(Table1,Table2)),"",VSTACK(Table1,EXPAND(Table2,,3,"")))		
Jack	36	78
Jill	87	
Amy	13	66
Janet	45	81
Ted	34	
Jane	56	
Mary		
Dan	17	

Figure 16-12. *That'll work: Defining datasets as tables calls upon EXPAND in order to remove the zeroes*

That slightly convoluted expression enables the user to enter new records that can be stacked, while at the same time exchanging blanks for the zeroes that will appear in blank cells at the outset. Bottom line: in this case we need EXPAND.

Summing Up

The preceding section addressed a problem that's peculiar to the VSTACK function, which stacks, or combines, different datasets into a new whole: the fact that it treats and returns blank cells as zeroes, disseminating a bit of misinformation which that encourage erroneous formula results as well. We've seen that the zeroes can be replaced by actual blanks, either when the data contributing to a VSTACK stand as conventional datasets, or when they've been tweaked into tables – in the former case *without* recourse to the EXPAND function, and in the latter case where EXPAND does seem to be required.

Now when all is said and done you may decide that, in light of the data-management roles played by EXPAND, you're not likely to use it very often anyway. Could be, but there's another, altogether different property of EXPAND that you may want – and need – to know about.

EXPAND and Unpivoting Data

If you remain unconvinced about the virtues of EXPAND, we'll see now that it can add crucial value to a formula-based solution to what is nowadays called the unpivoting of data.

To explain, by turning to an illustration drawn from the *EXPAND – pivoting data* practice file, the unpivoting process reconfigures a dataset looking like this familiar set of exam results retrieved by Figure 16-13.

name	soc	phil	poli sci	art	physics	chem
Bill	75	90	89	72	89	79
Dana	55	68	87	47	56	50
Ed	61	38	46	36	88	66
Jack	34	80	81	56	57	64
Jane	66	83	30	72	66	56
Hortense	41	85	53	75	90	45
Paul	71	59	69	61	100	72
Ted	66	66	70	35	76	91
Ulysses	59	52	100	94	38	31
Wanda	84	97	35	52	75	86
Barry	45	45	43	100	78	43

Figure 16-13. *Subject(s) to change: each subject occupies its own field*

to one that looks like this (in excerpt), reported in Figure 16-14.

Name	Subject	Score
Bill	soc	75
Bill	phil	90
Bill	poli sci	89
Bill	art	72
Bill	physics	89
Bill	chem	79
Dana	soc	55
Dana	phil	68
Dana	poli sci	87
Dana	art	47
Dana	physics	56
Dana	chem	50

Figure 16-14. *Narrowing the field(s): to three, to be exact. The data are the same, though*

(The student names have been range-named stu, the subjects sub, and the test scores sc.)

The intentional shrinkage of the original data from seven to three fields – and without any elimination of data - bespeaks a textbook case of unpivoting. To be sure, "unpivoting" is a mildly inaccurate term, because the data here *haven't* been submitted to an actual pivot table, and in fact one *can't* unpivot the data captured in a pivot table. What "unpivoting" really means to say is that data to be unpivoted resemble a conventional pivot table *result*, by its data organization and arrangement of fields; unpivoting a dataset, then, is a means for dragging the data back a few steps and making them pivot-table ready – that is, fit to *be* pivot tabled. (Note that a command-based means for unpivoting can be performed by Excel's Power Query Editor.)

Central in our case to the unpivoting process is a collecting of all the subject names into one field as we see above, each entry accompanied by a specific score and the student who achieved it. Because our dataset features 66 test scores, the corresponding student name and subject fields must also contain 66 entries once they're unpivoted – even though the original dataset records the eleven student names and six subjects only *once* each. And here's where the EXPAND function comes in – it can reproduce the student names and the subjects the desired number of times and, with the cooperation of the TOCOL function, pour the results down a single column – that is, into a single, unpivoted field.

EXPANDing Its Horizons

So far, we've instructed EXPAND to perform some limited expansions – that is, we've asked it to swell a two-column dataset by one column, for example, as recollected by Figure 16-15.

Name	ID	
Ted	34	
Jane	56	
Mary	12	
Dan	17	
=EXPAND(D9:E12,,3)		
Ted	34	#N/A
Jane	56	#N/A
Mary	12	#N/A
Dan	17	#N/A

Figure 16-15. *Three on two: expanding a dataset by one column again*

But EXPAND needn't restrict itself to a one-column increment. It's perfectly possible to write

=EXPAND(D9:D12,,10)

(Note we've omitted the "pad with argument, and here we're expanding just one column of data.)

That formula yields the following, in Figure 16-16.

=EXPAND(D9:D12,,10)								
Ted	#N/A	#N/A	#N/A	#N/A	#N/A	#N/A	#N/A	#N/A	#N/A
Jane	#N/A	#N/A	#N/A	#N/A	#N/A	#N/A	#N/A	#N/A	#N/A
Mary	#N/A	#N/A	#N/A	#N/A	#N/A	#N/A	#N/A	#N/A	#N/A
Dan	#N/A	#N/A	#N/A	#N/A	#N/A	#N/A	#N/A	#N/A	#N/A

Figure 16-16. *Nah, we don't want #N/A*

All of which asks the obvious question anew, reprising the one we posed earlier in the chapter: why would I want to write such an expression?

Well, you probably wouldn't, but with some prudent fixes, formulas such as the preceding one can be made to *copy a range of values* multiple times, particularly ranges consisting of one column or row. And that means that EXPAND can take our eleven student names and explode them into the 66 instances we need.

In order to clone the eleven student names into the requisite 66, we can begin by writing the following formula in cell K6:

=IFNA(EXPAND(stu,,6),stu)

And that yields the following, per Figure 16-17.

=IFNA(EXPAND(stu,,6),stu)					
Bill	Bill	Bill	Bill	Bill	Bill
Dana	Dana	Dana	Dana	Dana	Dana
Ed	Ed	Ed	Ed	Ed	Ed
Jack	Jack	Jack	Jack	Jack	Jack
Jane	Jane	Jane	Jane	Jane	Jane
Hortense	Hortense	Hortense	Hortense	Hortense	Hortensi
Paul	Paul	Paul	Paul	Paul	Paul
Ted	Ted	Ted	Ted	Ted	Ted
Ulysses	Ulysses	Ulysses	Ulysses	Ulysses	Ulysses
Wanda	Wanda	Wanda	Wanda	Wanda	Wanda
Barry	Barry	Barry	Barry	Barry	Barry

Figure 16-17. *11 x 6: 66 names – courtesy of EXPAND, with a little help from IFNA*

(Thanks to Excel boffin Mike Girvin for the formula streamlining tip.)

Of course, that output begs for some explanation. We've already seen that EXPAND augments, or expands, a range with additional columns – whose cells display the #N/A message by default. Thus, left to its own devices, this formula

$$=EXPAND(stu,,6)$$

would wreak the scenario that's snapshot by Figure 16-18.

=EXPAND(stu,,6)					
Bill	#N/A	#N/A	#N/A	#N/A	#N/A
Dana	#N/A	#N/A	#N/A	#N/A	#N/A
Ed	#N/A	#N/A	#N/A	#N/A	#N/A
Jack	#N/A	#N/A	#N/A	#N/A	#N/A
Jane	#N/A	#N/A	#N/A	#N/A	#N/A
Hortense	#N/A	#N/A	#N/A	#N/A	#N/A
Paul	#N/A	#N/A	#N/A	#N/A	#N/A
Ted	#N/A	#N/A	#N/A	#N/A	#N/A
Ulysses	#N/A	#N/A	#N/A	#N/A	#N/A
Wanda	#N/A	#N/A	#N/A	#N/A	#N/A
Barry	#N/A	#N/A	#N/A	#N/A	#N/A

Figure 16-18. *55 unavailable names*

But the IFNA function, a dedicated IF statement for the #N/A message, stands watch over EXPAND and replaces any column loaded with #N/As with the data from the original range stu. But at the same time, IFNA sees to it that if a column *is* free of #N/As, the nested formula – EXPAND(stu,,6) – takes over, and returns stu. Thus, with IFNA in charge, you get the data from stu whether or not the #N/As are in force.

Note that the value 66 – the total number of student name entries we require – is the product of the number of students (eleven) times the number of subjects (six), and so our formula could also be written

$$=IFNA(EXPAND(stu,,COUNTA(sub)),stu)$$

We're Almost There

But either way, we're not finished. Remember that we want the newly returned 66 student names to descend one column, and line themselves up with the like-numbered test scores. Right now, however, the names are pulling across six columns. You may be able to surmise what's coming next: we'll put in a call to the TOCOL function:

=TOCOL(IFNA(EXPAND(stu,,6),stu))

That cinches all the student-name data in single-column formation (in excerpt), as displayed in Figure 16-19.

=TOCOL(IFNA(EXPAND(stu,,6),stu))			
Bill			
Bill			
Bill			
Bill			
Bill			
Bill			
Dana			
Dana			
Dana			
Dana			
Dana			
Dana			
Ed			
Ed			
Ed			
Ed			
Ed			

Figure 16-19. *Students in single file*

Now we can do much the same for the subject data. Hop into L6 and write

=TOCOL(IFNA(EXPAND(sub,11),sub))

and that formula unfurls (in excerpt), per Figure 16-20.

	=TOCOL(IFNA(EXPAND(sub,11),sub))				
Bill	soc				
Bill	phil				
Bill	poli sci				
Bill	art				
Bill	physics				
Bill	chem				
Dana	soc				
Dana	phil				
Dana	poli sci				
Dana	art				
Dana	physics				
Dana	chem				
Ed	soc				
Ed	phil				
Ed	poli sci				
Ed	art				
Ed	physics				
Ed	chem				

Figure 16-20. *Class assembly: each student is matched to each subject*

Now compare the two formulas:

=TOCOL(IFNA(EXPAND(stu,,6),stu))

=TOCOL(IFNA(EXPAND(sub,11),sub))

Note the subtle but essential difference that sets them apart. The first EXPAND expression posts a *comma* in lieu of the number of rows, meaning that EXPAND invokes the eleven student rows by default and then moves on to the requested six-column reference. But the second formula has to *specify* eleven rows, because the subject data runs *horizontally* across a single row; and so this time EXPAND needs to be told how many rows we require. Its column argument – six – is omitted by default, as is the row argument for the student names. Thus, the second formula, minus TOCOL

=IFNA(EXPAND(sub,11),sub)

would result, as in Figure 16-21.

=IFNA(EXPAND(sub,11),sub)					
soc	phil	poli sci	art	physics	chem
soc	phil	poli sci	art	physics	chem
soc	phil	poli sci	art	physics	chem
soc	phil	poli sci	art	physics	chem
soc	phil	poli sci	art	physics	chem
soc	phil	poli sci	art	physics	chem
soc	phil	poli sci	art	physics	chem
soc	phil	poli sci	art	physics	chem
soc	phil	poli sci	art	physics	chem
soc	phil	poli sci	art	physics	chem
soc	phil	poli sci	art	physics	chem

Figure 16-21. *Changing the subjects: eleven rows by request, six columns by default. Remember the source data consists of one row and six columns.*

Because the student and subject data proceed vertically and horizontally, respectively, the student results reveal one name per row, while the subjects transmit one subject name per *column*.

You'll be happy to know that the final field in our unpivot exercise is the easiest to navigate. In M6, all you need write

=TOCOL(sc)

culminating in the following (in excerpt) via Figure 16-22.

		=TOCOL(sc)
Bill	soc	75
Bill	phil	90
Bill	poli sci	89
Bill	art	72
Bill	physics	89
Bill	chem	79
Dana	soc	55
Dana	phil	68
Dana	poli sci	87
Dana	art	47
Dana	physics	56
Dana	chem	50
Ed	soc	61
Ed	phil	38
Ed	poli sci	46
Ed	art	36
Ed	physics	88
Ed	chem	66

Figure 16-22. *It's all over but the headers*

That simple formula works because the test scores *already* total 66 in number, and hence that number need not be expanded. All we need to do is to line the values up in a single column, which is precisely what TOCOL is all about.

Note as well that all this formulaic activity keeps the data in sync: Bill's scores match up perfectly with his subjects, as they do for all the students.

The next and final step is to enter three headers above the columns, and your pivot table awaits – with one important caution: pivot tables are typically initiated by simply clicking any cell in the dataset, but here, because each field stands as a distinct spill range, you need to fire up the pivot table by clicking one of the header names. Doing so ensures that all the data will be pivoted.

For Extra Credit...

And now if you're feeling *really* adventurous, you could pack all of the above into one grand mega-formula, ready to leap into action with some generous help from HSTACK:

=HSTACK(TOCOL(IFNA(EXPAND(stu,,6),stu)),

TOCOL(IFNA(EXPAND(sub,11),sub)),TOCOL(sc))

And that, ladies and gentlemen, is a real dynamic array formula.

Index

A, B

Array, 1, 65
    character count, 4, 5
    character-summing formula, 6–8
    dynamic arrays, 23–39
    dynamic development, 6
    dynamic functions, 8
    formulas, 5
        assessment, 15
        character-count-summing, 9
        constants, 18
        horizontal alignment, 19
        IF function, 14
        keystrokes, 11, 12
        LARGE function, 20
        legendary sequence, 11
        lifting, 11
        one-formula grader, 13–17
        operations, 10
        re-oriented process, 19
        reputation, 9
        rule information, 10
        squiggly formations, 11
        SUM function, 9
        vertical orientation, 20
        VLOOKUP formula, 17–19
        workaround, 20
    implicit intersection, 7
    multiple values, 5
    testing process, 3
    UNIQUE, 53
    VLOOKUP function, 2
    word processor, 4
    working definition
        AVERAGE/MAX/COUNT
            function, 2
        elementary illustration, 2
        formulas, 2
        spreadsheet, 1
        VLOOKUP function, 3, 4
AVERAGE function
    DROP function, 203, 204

C

CHOOSECOLS and CHOOSEROWS
    functions, 171
    blank rows, 192
    dataset process, 191, 192
    error message, 184
    essential arguments, 181
    EXPAND function, 187
    formatting issues, 185
    formula, 186
    odd-numbered dataset rows, 192
    record-braking, 187–189
    resequencing fields, 183
    row count entries, 189
    salesperson data, 182
    sort index argument, 183, 184
    table information, 186
    TAKE/DROP functions, 193
    three-column structure, 187
    UNIQUE function, 189–191

© Abbott Ira Katz 2023
A. I. Katz, *Up Up and Array!*, https://doi.org/10.1007/978-1-4842-8966-2

U

Printed in the United States
by Baker & Taylor Publisher Services